# Cambridge Elements

Elements in Shakespeare and Text
edited by
Claire M. L. Bourne
*The Pennsylvania State University*
Rory Loughnane
*University of Kent*

# SHAKESPEARE AND SCALE

*The Archive of Early Printed English*

Anupam Basu
*Washington University in St Louis*

Shaftesbury Road, Cambridge CB2 8EA, United Kingdom

One Liberty Plaza, 20th Floor, New York, NY 10006, USA

477 Williamstown Road, Port Melbourne, VIC 3207, Australia

314–321, 3rd Floor, Plot 3, Splendor Forum, Jasola District Centre,
New Delhi – 110025, India

103 Penang Road, #05–06/07, Visioncrest Commercial, Singapore 238467

Cambridge University Press is part of Cambridge University Press & Assessment,
a department of the University of Cambridge.

We share the University's mission to contribute to society through the pursuit of
education, learning and research at the highest international levels of excellence.

www.cambridge.org
Information on this title: www.cambridge.org/9781009306713

DOI: 10.1017/9781009306676

© Anupam Basu 2025

This publication is in copyright. Subject to statutory exception and to the provisions
of relevant collective licensing agreements, no reproduction of any part may take
place without the written permission of Cambridge University Press & Assessment.

When citing this work, please include a reference to the DOI 10.1017/9781009306676

First published 2025

*A catalogue record for this publication is available from the British Library*

ISBN 978-1-009-30671-3 Paperback
ISSN 2754-4257 (online)
ISSN 2754-4249 (print)

Cambridge University Press & Assessment has no responsibility for the persistence
or accuracy of URLs for external or third-party internet websites referred to in this
publication and does not guarantee that any content on such websites is, or will
remain, accurate or appropriate.

# Shakespeare and Scale

## The Archive of Early Printed English

Elements in Shakespeare and Text

DOI: 10.1017/9781009306676
First published online: April 2025

---

### Anupam Basu
*Washington University in St Louis*

Author for correspondence: Anupam Basu, prime.lens@gmail.com

ABSTRACT: Scale has been the central promise of the digital turn. The creation of corpora such as EEBO and EEBO-TCP has eased the logistics of access to primary sources for scholars of Shakespeare and early English literature and culture and fundamentally altered the ways in which we retrieve, read, think about, and analyze texts. However, the large-scale curation of historical corpora poses unique challenges and requires scholarly insight and significant algorithmic intervention. In sections on "Text," "Corpus," "Search," and "Discovery," this Element problematizes the specific affordances of computation and scale as primary conceptual categories rather than incidental artifacts of digitization. From text-encoding and search to corpus-scale data visualization and machine-learning, it discusses a range of computational techniques that can facilitate corpus curation and enable exploratory, experimental modes of discovery that not only serve as tools to ease access but accommodate and respond to the demands of humanistic inquiry.

KEYWORDS: digital, Shakespeare, archive, curation, book history

© Anupam Basu 2025

ISBNs: 9781009306713 (PB), 9781009306676 (OC)
ISSNs: 2754-4257 (online), 2754-4249 (print)

# Contents

| | | |
|---|---|---|
| 1 | Theory: Text | 1 |
| 2 | Theory: Corpus | 23 |
| 3 | Praxis: Search | 45 |
| 4 | Praxis: Discovery | 77 |

## 1 Theory: Text

The impact of digital media on early modern studies in general, and editorial scholarship in particular, has been long and profound. From scanned facsimiles to editions of single texts or authors to large-scale, transcribed corpora like the Early English Books Online – Text Creation Partnership (EEBO-TCP), the ease of access and flexibility offered by digital texts has transformed everyday research and pedagogical practices. Especially in the field of scholarly editing, the anticipation and acceptance of digital texts has a long prehistory.[1] Textual studies embraced and theorized the possibilities of digital texts quite early and shaped significant aspects of technological development that paved the way for the creation of massive archives of digital media. The development of TEI (Text Encoding Initiative), first as an SGML (Standard Generalized Markup Language) and then as an XML (Extensible Markup Language) protocol, was at the forefront of this innovation and influenced technologies that would be at the core of the World Wide Web and the explosion of the internet.[2]

Thanks to multidecade, multi-institution digitization projects such as the EEBO-TCP, early modern scholarship finds itself in the unique position that the vast majority of the texts it covers as a field are now available in

---

[1] For an early example of corpus scale scholarship, often described as the first digital humanities project, see R. Busa, "The Annals of Humanities Computing: The Index Thomisticus," *Computers and the Humanities* 14, no. 2 (1980): 83–90. For early articulations of the possibilities offered by digital texts, see Peter L. Shillingsburg, *Scholarly Editing in the Computer Age: Theory and Practice* (Athens: University of Georgia Press, 1986), and Jerome J. McGann, *The Textual Condition* (Princeton: Princeton University Press, 1991). Sukanta Chaudhuri, *The Metaphysics of Text* (Cambridge: Cambridge University Press, 2010), offers a nuanced overview how digital texts have broadened the theoretical horizons of scholarly editing.

[2] Nancy Ide and C. M. Sperberg-Mcqueen, "The Text Encoding Initiative: Its History, Goals, and Future Development," *Computers and the Humanities* 29, no. 1 (1995): 5–15.

a searchable digital format.³ Moreover, Shakespeare's texts have held a privileged position even within the broader field of early modern studies and have been among the earliest ones available in well-curated digital versions.⁴ The availability of texts, combined with the broader accessibility of Shakespeare, has spurred computational work and served as testing grounds for many digital humanities methodologies. Perhaps the most publicly visible intervention of this steady stream of digital and quantitative scholarship has been the use of stylometric analysis in the *New Oxford Shakespeare* edition to make radical claims about the authorship of several plays.⁵ The initial hum of excitement about digital texts, therefore, has grown into a veritable roar over the last two decades. No aspect of early modern scholarly work – from editing and research to pedagogy and performance, from text encoding and bibliographic research to stylometrics and cultural analytics – remains untouched by digital technology.

But a lingering anxiety continues to mark this encounter with technology. Neither the pervasive presence of digital texts in everyday scholarly practice nor the depth and vitality of scholarship spurred by digital technology can alleviate the note of uncertainty, perhaps even apprehension, that remains in many assessments of its impact. On the one hand, many digital techniques and strategies are deeply familiar, and their use in scholarly practice – especially in the field of scholarly editing – is so ingrained that they present well-traversed territory. And yet, the flexibility and scalability of digital texts that make them

---

³ "Early English Books Online – Text Creation Partnership," http://quod.lib.umich.edu/e/eebogroup/ (accessed April 21, 2023). I will return to the question of EEBO-TCP's coverage later, but it is worth noting that while it is certainly comprehensive enough to accommodate most research and teaching as well as statistical analysis, it is not quite a randomly sampled dataset and, in addition to certain editorial preferences, echoes the exigencies of book history and survival rates.

⁴ For a brief overview of early digital editions, see Toby Malone and Brett Greatley-Hirsch, "Digital Shakespeare," in Paula Rabinowitz, ed., *Oxford Research Encyclopedia of Literature*, 2021, https://doi.org/10.1093/acrefore/9780190201098.013.1192.

⁵ Gary Taylor and Gabriel Egan, eds., *The New Oxford Shakespeare: Authorship Companion*, 1st ed. (Oxford: Oxford University Press, 2017).

such a valuable resource also raise some concerns. Suzanne Gossett, in her discussion of "Textual Studies After the Digital Turn" in *Shakespeare and Textual Theory*, gestures at this sense of unease in terms of the fast-changing and disorienting nature of the technological terrain. She notes that even though her coda on the "immaterial text" and its role in Shakespeare scholarship was written last, it will likely be the first to be outdated. The move to digital media, she suggests, "has caused considerable disruption and has radically altered the communication circuit," even as she acknowledges the great impact of technology – "both theoretical and practical" – on scholarly editing. She points to "concerns about the loss of intellectual accuracy," and notes that new tools and techniques pose significant challenges for "traditional Shakespeare scholars."[6] Interestingly, Gossett admits that textual scholarship has always required scholars to master somewhat esoteric skillsets, such as "creating collation formulas, tracing the reuse of skeleton formes, or operating a Hinman collator."[7] What, then, one might ask, is so unique about the challenges presented by digital technologies? Why do digital texts, which have been around, and well theorized, for decades now, continue to evoke such a wide range of reservations?

In this Element, I intend to interrogate the sense of the uncanny – a deeply unsettling strangeness within familiar terrain – that haunts this anxious relationship with the digital. By rethinking our underlying assumptions about digital texts and computation, I suggest, we can open up new ways of exploring individual texts and their place within the broader corpus – ways that transcend mere automation and can accommodate fundamentally humanistic modes of thinking. In this section I argue that while contemporary editorial practice has wholeheartedly embraced the flexibility offered by digital texts, it has not come to terms with such texts as truly computational objects – objects that are not mere electronic proxies of material texts but uniquely flexible computational artifacts in their own right. Editorial theory has paid attention to the ways in which the digital

---

[6] Suzanne Gossett, *Shakespeare and Textual Theory*, The Arden Shakespeare (London: Bloomsbury Publishing, 2022), 215.

[7] Gossett, *Shakespeare and Textual Theory*, 217.

format makes it possible to capture the complexities and inherent instability of the processes of textual transmission. However, by treating texts as computational objects, I want to emphasize their affordances in a fundamentally new medium. We often treat such affordances as happy byproducts of the electronic format, something the digital medium innately lends itself to: search, retrieval, enumeration. In other words, these problems are transferred to the domain of technical implementation rather than humanistic conceptualization. The next section, expanding our scope from "text" to "corpus," foregrounds computation as not only a set of strictly procedural goal-oriented processes, but as a heuristic that enables transmutability, intertextuality, and scalability, and that explores the ways in which conceptualizations of scale overlap with humanistic modes of enquiry.

The final two sections – "Search" and "Discovery" – explore related but, I shall argue, fundamentally distinct modes of information retrieval that we associate with computation. While "search" seems to be a deeply familiar paradigm in a world where we are inundated with information, my purpose is to render it somewhat strange. By dissecting examples of certain kinds of search that scholars encounter regularly – either for catalogs or for, say, the ProQuest EEBO website – I highlight the complex and often messy historical trajectories and intellectual assumptions that mediate what might at first glance appear to be a thoroughly dry, technical process. Having problematized the concept of search, or at least rendered it less stable than a mere technological black box that simply retrieves bits of information, I extend my study of its possibilities under the rubric of "discovery" to accommodate a set of approaches that are more open ended, flexible, and, often, serendipitous. These approaches, I argue, have the potential not only to align with but also to extend humanistic modes of inquiry and transform the kinds of questions we can ask of the early modern corpus in the first place. To be sure, such approaches can often be highly technical, involving statistical modeling, data mining, and machine learning. Nevertheless, I shall argue that breaking away from static notions of text and corpus and seeing computation not only as a mere technological handmaiden but also as a distinctive mode of knowledge reveals affinities with the kinds of subtlety, ambiguity, and intertextuality that humanists value. It is a phenomenon that requires distinctive kinds of scholarly attention, and it has the potential not only to align with but also to extend humanistic modes of inquiry and transform the kinds of questions we can ask of the early modern corpus in the first place. Throughout this Element, I will distinguish and disturb terms that are usually collapsed together or implicitly treated as slightly different ends of the same spectrum: digital/computational; text/corpus; editing/curating. My intention in troubling these binaries is not to suggest some kind of qualitative/quantitative divide or fundamental incommensurability between the humanistic scrutiny that individual texts invoke and the technological apparatus required to make large numbers of texts tractable to computation. In fact, I hope to show that these terms denote not so many different objects or activities but distinct and complementary perspectives, each with its unique scholarly purchase. Only by reconciling these perspectives – by seeing what is distinctive about scale and computation as modes of humanistic (rather than technical) knowledge – can we begin to undo the strange unfamiliarity at the heart of our encounter with digital textuality.

## *Digital Text*

From its very outset, the appeal of digital texts has been their highly procedural and hierarchical nature. Computers are good at implementing well-defined repeatable procedures and were deemed ideal for taking over what Peter Shillingsburg called the "idiot work" of scholarly editing: "tedious jobs ... most liable to careless error," such as "collation, typesetting, and proofreading."[8] But the excitement of handing over such tasks was tempered by concerns about computers ultimately overstepping these mechanical bounds and somehow infringing on the more critical aspects of scholarly editing. Poststructuralist re-evaluations of textual theory and the critiques of the New Bibliography it has produced have helped to renegotiate this hierarchy between the procedural and the critical. The editor is no longer – or as explicitly – tasked with "critical analysis" or with teasing out some unique insight about authorial intention. Freed from this burden, scholarly editing has become more collaborative, enlisting the reader as a participant in the critical process of negotiating the problems of textual transmission rather than aspiring toward an ideal, fixed text. This paradigmatic shift has been

---

[8] Shillingsburg, *Scholarly Editing in the Computer Age*, 135.

facilitated in part by the malleability and fluidity of the digital medium, which makes it possible for the text to be radically multiple.[9] As Kathryn Sutherland puts it, the "digital vantage point" allows the shifting of interpretive agency that was silently assumed by the New Bibliographers.[10] Gossett has suggested that the flexibility of digital editions facilitates the ideals of the "postmodern edition" and makes it possible to represent "the challenge of poststructuralism to any concept of textual stability."[11]

These are lofty aspirations for what an electronic edition should be, though often tempered by skepticism about the underlying technology's ability to accommodate critical nuance. This tension between liberatory embrace and apprehension has been the driving dialectic of modern textual scholarship's encounter with digital technology. Digital editions require relatively complex technical, financial, and institutional infrastructures to create and maintain. But what makes the digital medium so appealing to scholarly editors, and also what provides a conceptual vantage point from which to contemplate textuality itself, is a core set of technologies that are in themselves elegantly simple: XML and hypertext. Both are, in fact, information organization protocols that make use of more generalizable underlying text or data-processing technologies. An XML or hypertext file or data-stream is no different from any other stream of text information that computer processing, storage, and transmission hardware can handle. Of course, the "simplicity" I attribute to this innovation is deceptive. We need only remind ourselves of the explosion that the addition of hyperlinks to previously text-based networks caused in the form of the World Wide Web to realize that immensely complex systems can be built out of strikingly simple core innovations.

---

[9] For examples of digital projects that foreground the polyvalent nature of texts, see "The James Merrill Digital Archive: Materials for The Book of Ephraim," accessed May 13, 2024, http://omeka.wustl.edu/omeka/exhibits/show/james merrillarchive/; "Bichitra: Online Tagore Variorum," accessed May 13, 2024, https://bichitra.jdvu.ac.in/index.php.

[10] Kathryn Sutherland, "Being Critical: Paper Based Editing and the Digital Environment," in *Text Editing, Print and the Digital World*, ed. Marilyn Deegan and Kathryn Sutherland (Farnham: Ashgate, 2009), 16.

[11] Gossett, *Shakespeare and Textual Theory*, 218.

The appeal of both these protocols lies in the ways they can break both the linearity and the transparency of the textual encounter: XML introduces organizing structures to texts as markup, paratextual information in the form of metadata, and the ability to encode multiple versions or states of text. Hypertext, on the other hand, punctuates the linearity of text flow without quite dismantling it. It puts at the reader's disposal the text's potential axes of connection and cross-pollination to its various outsides, and signals that every text exists within a larger matrix of material and cultural conditions. It is not difficult to see, even from such a schematic outline, why such an information architecture would seem liberating to editorial scholars who have always worked within the limitations of the printed codex. Even though print as a technology has, over its long history, developed a formidable array of apparatuses that reconfigure linear reading – notes, marginalia, indices, tables, concordances – the representation of multiple states and nonlinear organization still seem like convoluted accommodations rather than primary affordances of print.

The information infrastructure available in the digital space provides editors with the building blocks for moving from a notion of the text as some abstracted version of an originary stable object to an account of textuality as process. Electronic editions, in other words, are models of textual phenomena rather than representations of particular instantiations. One might suspect that, now that the editor is no longer burdened with divining authorial intention and can recruit the reader to navigate the labyrinth of textual states and variations, they might assume the more limited role of collator of evidence. It would be fair to say that technological innovation – the emergence of the editor as model-builder – has inspired (and, in turn, been spurred by) increasingly sophisticated theorizations of textuality, each challenging us to broaden our frameworks of textual analysis and the technical apparatus' capacity to accommodate ever more detail, ambiguity, and play.[12] If the editor's task is to capture what scholars

---

[12] See, for example, Elena Pierazzo, *Digital Scholarly Editing: Theories, Models and Methods*, 1st ed. (London: Routledge, 2015); and Katherine Bode, "The Difference an Editor Makes," *Modern Language Quarterly* 82, no. 3 (2021): 401–4.

like McKenzie and McGann have popularized as the processes of a text's "socialization," then they must attend not only to the text as a linguistic construct but also as an artifact mediated by multiple actors, processes, and materialities.[13] Shillingsburg's insistence that we further widen our conception of textual transmission to what he calls "script-acts" – which would include not only the customary sites of a text's socialization (editor, printer, publisher, bookseller, and so forth), but every interaction, including and especially readerly ones, that relate to texts – broadens this scope even further. A physical rendition of a text within such a framework is not only partial and necessarily provisional; it does not stand in any particularly privileged position. The emphasis rather lies on processes of textual encounter – creation, transmission, reception – which form an endless and ever-incomplete chain.

The road from textual authority to open-ended play, therefore, has been a fraught one that, in many ways, takes the ambit of play and polyvocality to its postmodern limits. Far from being relegated to the easily mechanizable "idiot work" of scholarly editing, an increasingly sophisticated machinery of textual representation seems to be evolving to meet the demands of even more astonishingly ambitious and nuanced conceptualizations of textuality. The expansiveness of the text-as-model paradigm puts ever-increasing pressure on the digital editions' capacity for representing ambiguity in ways that have made many editors anxious about losing sight of the original, somewhat pragmatic goals of scholarly editing. On the one hand, many have embraced the erosion of authority and argued that, once such absolute privileged insight is disavowed, the main utility of the digital text becomes its ability to demonstrate the unfixity of text and thus the contradictions inherent in its processes of production. Katherine Rowe termed such editions "good enough" texts, wherein textual instability offers an opportunity to renew the reader's engagement and intervention in the editorial process: "Yet new digital editions also invite us to return to editorial first principles, replacing single textual authorities with ambiguous

---

[13] D. F. McKenzie, *Bibliography and the Sociology of Texts* (Cambridge: Cambridge University Press, 1999); and Jerome J. McGann, "The Socialization of Texts," in *The Textual Condition* (Princeton: Princeton University Press, 2020), 69–87.

alternatives, and including the reader in the editorial process."[14] The moment of editorial intervention to fix a text in an apparently stable form no longer precedes, nor is separated from, the readerly encounter. Instead, reading subsumes within its hermeneutic instabilities the processes by which a text comes to be.

Despite being theoretically challenging and pedagogically productive, textual instability – and the radical celebration of it – also raises concerns. Thus, it is unsurprising to find that while Gossett shares some of Rowe's excitement about the opportunities provided by good-enough texts, she reminds us that textual editing remains a deeply pragmatic discipline, and that any theorization of text, however profoundly influenced by poststructuralist notions of epistemic fluidity and linguistic instability, must, in the last instance, be grounded in praxis. "Textual theory is different," she argues: "it focuses most often on developing an informed inference about the nature and history of a surviving text." It must be articulable in terms of formalized procedures of selection, elimination, and organization of various textual states. Gossett notes that while editors are aware that "philosophical premises are often implicit in textual work ... much textual theory is primarily concerned with methodology and procedure."[15] Digital editions give textual scholars the opportunity to "open up" the text, to invite the reader in as participant and co-creator in assessing the complex material and intellectual histories of transmission. But if the task of the editor is to be distinguished from that of the free-ranging literary theorist, the procedural foundations of textual editing need to be emphasized. One might say that the polarities of insightfully critical and merely procedural have been dissolved to an extent as the evolution of text technologies has proven that the digital text can rise to the challenges of literary reading.

---

[14] Katherine Rowe, "Living with Digital Incunables, or a 'Good-Enough' Shakespeare Text," in *Shakespeare and the Digital World: Redefining Scholarship and Practice*, ed. Christie Carson and Peter Kirwan (Cambridge: Cambridge University Press, 2014), 148.

[15] Gossett, *Shakespeare and Textual Theory*, 2–3.

## Computational Text

The text as model: an engine of meaning-making that carries within it the archaeology of its own material and social evolution. The metaphor is not quite a novel one. We are accustomed to thinking of the book as an evolving set of technologies that both facilitate and set limits on the production and circulation of language. Jerome McGann describes the book as "a machine of knowledge" and compares its capabilities with those of digital editions that he suggests can transcend "the formal limits of all hardcopy's informational and critical powers."[16] The electronic edition, McGann argues, opens up ways of interrupting hermeneutic procedures, urging us to encounter textuality as a generative process, as an unfolding performance of formal innovation: "electronic tools in literary studies don't simply provide a new point of view on the materials, they lift one's general level of attention to a higher order."[17]

The central point of thinking of the book as a machine is that, while it has metaphorical overtones (a book is *like* a machine in the way it amplifies and transforms ideas), it is also a literal description that draws attention to the materiality of the book. A book, as so much contemporary scholarship reminds us, is, first and foremost, a physical object, a technology of information. From the material intersection of paper, ink, thread, and glue to its conceptual innovations such as the random access the codex form facilitates, its easy reproducibility, and archival stability – the book doesn't merely supply a new template – a convenient technical upgrade from scroll and manuscript – it redefines our understanding of text. The technology of the book has imprinted itself invisibly on our notion of what a text can be.

It might seem that the text-as-machine comparison would be more obvious in the case of electronic texts, and we would not need to belabor it. After all, our basic access to such texts depends on our ability to negotiate considerably more complex piles of metal and plastic, not to mention the bewildering array of information transactions that Matthew G. Kirschenbaum

---

[16] Jerome McGann, *Radiant Textuality* (New York: Palgrave, 2004), 1153, 1201, Kindle edition.

[17] McGann, *Radiant Textuality*, 1173.

has described as the "cross-pollination of different services, platforms, and file formats."[18] Each of these layers shapes the possibilities and affordances of the digital text. From the material constraints that determine the limits of hardware – storage capacity, bandwidth, access times – to the more abstract levels of protocols, data structures, and algorithms that are stacked on them, these layers combine in intricate ways not only to determine how we access a text, but also to suggest all of the potential representations and transformations such a text might lend itself to. Scholars such as Kirschenbaum have reminded us of the inherent materiality of the "intense and intimate and at times fraught" collaborations of multiple layers of hardware and software that make digital texts possible.[19] From hard-drive spindles surfing nanometer-thick cushions of air, to bits traveling down complex network infrastructures, to pixels on the screen, Kirschenbaum's work paints a complex picture of the material amalgamations through which an abstraction such as a digital text can emerge.[20] Others, such as Lev Manovich and Yuk Hui, have attended to conceptual structures such as the database and networks as organizing principles that mediate our access to digital information.[21]

In drawing a distinction between the digital text and what I call a computational text, I want to sharpen this theoretical insight and attend to the text both as actual, material manifestation, and potential abstraction. An electronic text appears to us as a relatively stable object – usually seen on a screen through the hierarchical logic of text encoding protocols. We can trace the material and software transactions required to store, access, or manipulate it. But to attend to it as a primarily computational object is to see it in a state of radical flux – never settled into what we might think of as

---

[18] Matthew G. Kirschenbaum, *Bitstreams: The Future of Digital Literary Heritage*, Material Texts (Philadelphia: University of Pennsylvania Press, 2021), 5.

[19] Kirschenbaum, *Bitstreams*, 4.

[20] Matthew G. Kirschenbaum, *Mechanisms: New Media and the Forensic Imagination* (Cambridge, MA: MIT Press, 2012); *Track Changes: A Literary History of Word Processing* (Cambridge, MA: Harvard University Press, 2016); and *Bitstreams*.

[21] Lev Manovich, "Database as a Genre of New Media," *AI & Society* 14, no. 2 (2000): 176–83; and Yuk Hui, *On the Existence of Digital Objects* (Minneapolis: University of Minnesota Press, 2016), 109–49.

a native representation, some essential stable substrate over which other transformations are built. Instead, its material realizations are already highly algorithmically mediated transformations of an abstract logical state. For example, what might seem like a stream of text or XML to us would take drastically different shapes depending on whether it is stored on disc, loaded in memory, or transmitted through a network. Platforms, file systems, and protocols will determine the exact layout of bits and bytes that appear transcoded on our screen under the guise of a unified text. Whether we want to read the text, count up its words, or parse it as a tree of nested tags will determine what data structure or schema it might be best suited to. This extended paraphernalia of technical representations is usually conveniently hidden away from us. We are happy to encounter an appropriately stable rendition of the text in a word processor or browser – or, if we are technically inclined, to look under the hood at XML or its database representation. But to think of the text as a fundamentally computational object is to notice that renditions of the text are only provisional, arbitrary, and fungible transformations of an underlying logical entity. The "text," therefore, is always already in some state of flux, constantly unmade and remade to fit particular representational needs. Every interaction serves as an intervention in the latent state of the text. Each keystroke, each touchscreen scroll, each search operation leverages some unique transformation of the underlying logical object that is manipulated under the constraints of hardware and software or the efficiencies of algorithmic time and space.[22]

To think of a digital text as a manifestation of such an underlying computational text is to enable precisely the kinds of flexibility that literary scholars value. But, by and large, concerns about the internal technical dynamics of the text remain invisible to us and are rarely theorized. If we do pay attention to the technical dimensions of the text, it is in its relatively stable intermediate schematizations as XML encoding or a database table.

---

[22] Algorithmic complexity is reported in terms of the rate of increase in time of execution and memory space. For a basic introduction to algorithmic complexity, see Thomas H. Cormen, Charles E. Leiserson, Ronald L. Rivest, & Clifford Stein, *Introduction to Algorithms*, 4th ed. (Cambridge, MA: MIT Press, 2022).

There is more to this elision than a simple humanistic aversion or inability to negotiate the highly technical internal workings of a modern computer system. It is based on the tacit assumption that all the real or potential facilities of digital objects are inherent affordances of the digital form and do not need particular elaboration or theorization. In other words, we assume that computers are intrinsically capable of doing certain things, and the moment we have translated a text into some digital form, those affordances automatically fall into place. Even worse, this theoretical blindness is often precipitated on certain false equivalences between the processes of human attention and those of computational manipulation. The most persistent of these false equivalences in recent years has been the collapsing of fundamentally different modes of access to texts under the umbrella term "reading" – distant or close. But even when there is no explicit conflation of human and computational categories, we tend to assume that things like "search" are somehow transparent extrapolations of human forms of attention. That is, when a computer searches a text, it is essentially doing the equivalent of a human reader reading very, very fast – the only differences are the orders of magnitude in speed and the computer's immunity to tedium. This is not merely a naïve misunderstanding of a technical process; it has serious consequences for our work as critical readers and users of electronic textual archives.

The format of textual encoding is not coeval with all possible computational transformations of texts – it is merely the precondition of it. The kinds of generative transformation McGann attributes to electronic texts are not inherent properties of the text as a stable digital object; they are potential possibilities that arise out of making such an object "computable," as it were. A computational text, therefore, only exists as a mediated instantiation of an underlying principle of organization. It exists within the material constraints of hardware and the logical and algorithmic limits of software. It is also a text that always exists *in potentia*, in a state of radical flux – susceptible to any number of possible transformations and only accessible to us through such transformations. The original XML file that's loaded into memory is no more the "true" representation of the text than the tree-like xPath data model that lets us traverse its structure or retrieve particular "nodes." Nor is the transformation into a serial stream of words or "tokens" any more natural a representation of this text than when it is parsed into an index for searching or transformed into a vector for quantitative processing. All of these mutual states exist in relation to each other within a matrix of transformations that the logic of computation makes possible. As a comparison, we might think of some magical codex that contains within it the ability to transform into all its potential states, including states of disassembly. Imagine a material book that can transform from manuscript into various possible print formats, or into a variety of typographical and layout features, or grammatical and syntactical units, perhaps even to a distribution of individual typecases arranged in neat little piles, or into a heap of individual word magnets for the curious reader to rearrange and explore. We would possibly not call the disassembled forms of the First Folio a text. But it exists in a particular relationship to Shakespeare's text – one creates the other through a neatly procedural set of transformations. Set the letters in a precise and very complex order, and you get the First Folio. Disassemble them according to another logic, and you get a set of frequency counts that stand in a precise relationship to the text. To think of the First Folio as a computational text is to acknowledge the possibility that both versions are indeed transformations of the same underlying entity.

By imagining the radical possibilities of the electronic text and its affinities with the kinds of textual instability that scholars have cherished, we not only connect past critical practices to contemporary digitally mediated ones but also open up new ways of extending our framework from single texts to scalable intertextual ones. Jerome McGann and Lisa Samuels initiate a brilliant set of examples where they ask us to contemplate several poems in various states of "deformance."[23] The poems are radically transformed by the transposition or transformation of certain facets that we habitually take for granted in our encounter with language as a medium primarily geared toward "meaning". What would happen, McGann and Samuels ask, if we were to read a poem backward? What if we were to simply do away with lineation and encounter what was formally composed as poetry in the "deformed" shape of prose? Perhaps we might apply an even more drastic transformation and retain only the nouns or the verbs in

---

[23] Jerome McGann and Lisa Samuels, "Deformance and Interpretation," in *Radiant Textuality*, 2056.

*Shakespeare and Scale* 15

a poem, replacing every other word with empty spaces. The term "deformance," which they coin to describe this set of procedures of formal disassembly and eclectic reassembly, is an evocative one. It alludes, at once, to the notion of "defamiliarization," popularized by Russian Formalist critics such as Viktor Shklovsky as a central characteristic of literary language, as well as to the fact that such a process essentially envisions the textual encounter as performance. Each step in this set of experiments produces yet another unfamiliar projection of the poem – a transformed, distorted echo of the original text-object that invites us to shake off the burden of meaning-making as the dominant mode of encountering it. Instead, by disrupting grammar, syntax, and narrative, these experiments encourage us to explore other kinds of interconnectivity, patterns of sound and imagery that contribute to the poem's overall purchase as an aesthetic object. To be sure, throughout this process these poems still remain texts, and particularly literary texts – the exhilarating tour de force of speculative, deeply insightful reading McGann and Samuels produce in this chapter bears witness to that. In fact, it is because they are literary, McGann and Samuels argue, that we should be invested in their performative, generative dimensions rather than merely their denotative meaning.

McGann and Samuels' critical practice negotiates and seeks to undo what many might take to be an apparent opposition: between text as a humanistic object that celebrates uncertainty, ambiguity, and play and text as a computational object that is procedural, hierarchical, and schematic. McGann acknowledges that computational representation might, at its core, seem at odds with the "ambiguities and incommensurables" of humanistic reading: "Computational systems are ... designed to negotiate disambiguated, fully commensurable signifying structures."[24] This perceived contradiction between hermeneutic ambivalence and the structured, rigorous logic of computation has meant that such technology has been relegated to "technical and precritical occupations" such as "sorting, assessing, and disseminating" texts.[25] This disparity, McGann argues, reflects the tacit hierarchy between the critic/philosopher on the one hand and the scholar/

[24] McGann, *Radiant Textuality*, 121. [25] McGann, *Radiant Textuality*, 73.

editor on the other. The task of editing, being a grounded practice directed toward somewhat pragmatic ends, leans toward schematic, hierarchical representations – either as Lachmannian stemmata, typologies, or in the form of attention to the history of a text's layout and material transmission. In other words, editorial practice works toward the implementation of certain methodologies that, while embedded in a theoretical framework, are in themselves highly procedural and operationalizable. This aspect of editorial work lends itself easily to digital representation and is certainly one of the key reasons editorial scholarship has so freely embraced digital texts.

However, though in many aspects it echoes the prevailing optimism about digital texts that characterizes much of editorial theory in the last few decades, McGann's enthusiasm about the coming "complete editorial transformation of our inherited cultural archive" has certain crucially significant dimensions.[26] First, he argues that there is no contradiction between the strict proceduralism of digital texts and the free play of humanistic interpretation. In fact, his central intervention is to suggest that the attention to ambiguity and incommensurability that literary reading demands is, at its core, made possible by a set of highly procedural formal transformations. To pay attention to polyvalence, we must suspend, however momentarily, the dominance of grammatical meaning and allow other textures, other patterns and axes of connections to emerge. This is the core of his practice of "deformance": a text's generative possibilities emerge only by interrupting other kinds of hegemonic formal logics. But the ways in which such disruptions are affected consist of highly procedural transformations that lend themselves to what we might think of as algorithmic precision. In fact, all of the radical transformations that McGann and Samuels effect are easily implemented by anyone with even rudimentary text-processing skills. Thus, in McGann's conception, not only are the digital text's computational attributes not in contradiction with the demands of humanistic reading, they are the very conditions of it. He sees no contradiction between the iterative and the interpretive and suggests that, in time, such digital transformations will become "prosthetic extensions of [the] demand for critical reflection."[27]

---

[26] McGann, *Radiant Textuality*, 533. [27] McGann, *Radiant Textuality*, 536.

The conception of the text-as-machine pushes at this boundary between the well-defined schema and procedures of the text as a digital construct and the radical transformation such a text is capable of as a computational object. While he doesn't quite make the distinction between digital and computational, McGann imagines the text as embodying a kind of "quantum poetics" – a phrase that consciously juxtaposes scientific and creative registers.[28] In their co-written chapter McGann and Samuels develop, instead, an account of textuality as something that is always reducible to procedural formal interactions but whose effects, in aggregate, are fundamentally indeterminate and stochastic:

> Such a model brings to attention areas of the poetic and artifactual media that usually escape our scrutiny. But this enlargement of the subject matter of criticism doesn't define the most significant function of deformative operations. Far more important is the stochastic process it entails. Reading backward is a highly regulated method for disordering the senses of a text. It turns off the controls that organize the poetic system at some of its most general levels. When we run the deformative program through a particular work we cannot predict the results.[29]

The key purchase of the "quantum poetics" that McGann proposes is not to harness the reductive proceduralism of computation to the more versatile needs of humanistic reading. He seeks to utterly undo the opposition between scientific and humanistic, between procedure and play. In fact, one becomes the necessary precondition of the other.

## *Computation/Interpretation*

While McGann seems very aware that his collaborative experiments with Samuels have strong affinities to computational processes, he never explicitly formulates them as such. All of their "deformative" projections of texts

---

[28] McGann, *Radiant Textuality*, 145.

[29] McGann and Samuels, "Deformance and Interpretation," 2268.

could be generated computationally, but they do not articulate the procedures that would be involved in doing so. As a result, certain fundamental affordances of the computational approach are left unexplored. It is in the work of Stephen Ramsay that the computational and quantitative dimensions of deformance are finally examined in some detail. Ramsay's exploration of computation draws inspiration from McGann's deformative readings to put forward a manifesto for what he calls "algorithmic criticism."[30] It is a criticism that is conceived computationally from its very inception, but that seeks to undo certain fundamental assumptions about computation that are put forward by both critics and proponents of the approaches to textual analysis that have been termed "distant reading" or "cultural analytics." Such quantitative approaches, Ramsay argues, constitute "a hermeneutics that disallows the connotative and analogical methods of criticism," instead insisting on reproducibility, robustness, and statistical significance.[31]

To be sure, many computational methods make claims and use approaches where such accountability is necessary. However, Ramsay wants to leave room, within quantitative criticism, for the generative, rhetorical capabilities McGann celebrates in computational texts. He wants to resist the implied abandonment of the traditional rhetorical register of "persuasion" within which much humanistic scholarship operates and the inevitable slide into the surety of "proof" as the primary paradigm of quantitative reasoning. In other words, he seeks to retain continuity between the humanistic and the computational:

> If algorithmic criticism is to have a central hermeneutical tenet, it is this: that the narrowing constraints of computational logic – the irreducible tendency of the computer towards enumeration, measurement, and verification – is fully compatible with the goals of criticism.[32]

---

[30] Stephen Ramsay, *Reading Machines: Toward an Algorithmic Criticism* (Urbana-Champaign: University of Illinois Press, 2011).
[31] Ramsay, *Reading Machines*, 17.   [32] Ramsay, *Reading Machines*, 16.

The tangible procedures of computation – "the irreducible tendency of the computer towards enumeration, measurement, and verification" – do seem to present an irreconcilably different paradigm from that of literary reading, which is predicated on the very impossibility of absolute precision and the inevitable lapse of language into ambiguity and undecidability. But the seemingly reductive processes of quantification are no more than transformations of the underlying computational texts. Each neatly procedural and predictable step, when accumulated at scale, opens up deeply unfamiliar, generative, and, most importantly, fundamentally interpretive ways of looking at text.

Ramsay uses the example of using tf-idf scores to distinguish "important" words in a text. This is a widely used procedure in much text analysis and a standard part of any introductory textbook. But the formula doesn't represent any fundamental mathematical law or inherent statistical property of text; instead, it starts with an intuition and then builds layers of interpretive adjustments to it. What if we make the assumption that the more a word appears in a text, the more important we should consider it? A quick implementation of this – let's say on the corpus of Shakespeare's plays – will tell us that the most frequent words in Shakespeare are what are called "stop-words" that make up the syntactic mesh of language: "the," "and," "to," "my," "of," etcetera. Of course, this is to be expected. When we say a word is "important" or "characteristic" in a text, or even significant in a genre or authorial style, we do not simply mean frequent. Perhaps "distinctive" would be a better term to use: something that occurs disproportionately in a text. Notice that we are already creeping toward qualitative, interpretive categories. Disproportionate implies some conception of an expected normal rate of occurrence – and that requires some degree of linguistic and cultural competence. How do we quantitatively model this sense of distinctiveness? Having started with the number of occurrences of a word – term-frequency, denoted as $tf$ – we might now multiply it by a weight, $w$. So, if a play has n distinct words denoted as tokens $\{t_1, t_2 \ldots t_n\}$, we could compute a set of weights $\{w_1, w_2, \ldots w_n\}$, so that the product of the two $\{t_1 w_1, t_2 w_2 \ldots t_n w_n\}$ would be scores that are quantitative representations of the importance of any term $t_i$. To realize our goal, therefore, we have to come up with some computation for $w_i$ that will serve to amplify or diminish different categories of words. We want to give less weightage to words that are distributed across all texts and more to the ones that are gathered in a small number of texts. These latter ones are less likely to be mere syntactic words and more likely to be significant elements of the texts. Perhaps we can express this as a fraction: *df/N*: *df* being the "document frequency" of the word, the number of documents that have at least one instance of the word out of the total number of documents, *N*. Thus expanded, the formula becomes:

$$tfidf = tf_n \times \frac{N}{df_n}$$

Under this interpretation – and it is important to remember that, in spite of its formalized representation, this is an interpretation – a word like "the," which appears in every text, gets a weight of $w = N/df$ where both *N* and *df* are 1, so its weight is not amplified at all. Conversely, if a word appears in just one out of 36 plays, its weight is 36/1 – that is, it is amplified 36 times. It turns out that stop-words are so frequent that this amplification isn't enough in a small corpus of texts to elevate the importance of rarer words. So, let us change the formula for the weight slightly to adjust for this:

$$tfidf = tf_n \times log\left(\frac{N}{df_n}\right)$$

The schematic representation might be somewhat unfamiliar to our customary ways of thinking about what words or ideas are characteristic of literary texts. Indeed, the point I am trying to make about this simple computation could have been made without this formalization of the mathematical concept. But it is precisely this kind of formalization or quantitative logic that critics such as McGann, Samuels, and Ramsay want us to be responsive to. The formula, in spite of the fact that it lends itself to precise mathematical schematization, is not some immutable or "objective" law of language. It has many variations, each adapted to different interpretive purposes. In fact, Ramsay uses a slightly different version of this formula.

## Shakespeare and Scale

Our adjustment takes advantage of the fact that the logarithm of 1 is 0 – so any word so frequent that it appears in every or almost every text gets a 0 or near 0 weight. What remains are words that are relatively frequent and also somewhat unique to texts. Here are four Shakespeare plays represented by their most characteristic words, as computed by our revised tf-idf formula:

> toby malvolio cesario topas olivia andrew illyria madonna orsino
> cassius brutus caesar antony casca titinius messala octavius cinna
> ariel trinculo milan stephano naples prospero caliban gonzalo
>   tunis island
> cordelia regan edmund nuncle lear cornwall goneril edgar
>   gloucester kent

While it might be satisfying that our formula has picked up proper nouns specific to these plays (*Twelfth Night*, *Julius Caesar*, *The Tempest*, *King Lear*), this might be somewhat underwhelming in terms of generating insight. But if we eliminate names of characters, we start to get closer to something that looks like McGann's notion of deformance. Here again, are high tf-idf score keywords from some plays:

> shepherd forest verses clown heigh-ho
> jew ducats bond clerk christian
> handkerchief whore strumpet jealous turk
> fairy wall moonshine lovers wood
> daggers knocking tyrant sisters bubble
> niece stockings knight yellow fooling

We could still probably guess easily which plays these words are from, but this starts to approach the notion of a deformative reading whereby a set of regulated distortions transform a text into a form that forces us to attend to it in new ways and interrupts the usual ways of thinking about meaning, plot, narrative, etcetera. Much more can be done with this, with increasing degrees of quantitative and interpretive sophistication. We might decide that we are interested in themes or concepts instead of mere words and might transform the text using a topic model or semantic vectors. We might even extend the current formula to make it more nuanced about the distribution of words across texts and how it is captured in our variable, *df*.

The point of this exercise is not to mathematically compute some objective, irrefutable criteria of significant words in a play, much less to determine what a play is "really about." To fall into that illusion of objectivity is to lose sight of the fundamentally fungible conception of the computational text that only presents itself to us through some transformation. And we might argue that each transformation – even the ones where we feel we are reading the "unmediated" text on screen – is as arbitrary and interpretive as the other. It is up to us as editors, critics, and readers to decide which particular projection we might find useful to engage with.

The machine metaphor is worth returning to here. The text is always already a generative machine. The particular affordances of computation give us easy access to such sites of productive rupture. The logics of formal transformation produce altered projections of the texts that – reductive and highly distortive in themselves – prove to be fertile provocations, drawing us into textual encounters that are difficult to access within totalized renditions of the text-object. A word McGann uses to describe both books and digital texts as different orders of machines is "prosthetic" – something that extends or enhances our reach and provides access to what already exists but is difficult to access. But a machine is also something that transforms and remakes. The radical transformative quality of the text as generative machine is much more than a prosthetic – a mere revealing of what is within. Like the evocative cultural politics of the famous inscription on Woodie Guthrie's guitar – "this machine kills fascists" – the promise of the machine is almost quasi-mystical. It promises a transformation that is irreducible to any set of causal steps. In the cultural imaginary, the machine embodies a set of contradictions. It is deeply procedural – made up of levers and pulleys, or circuits and logic boards locked in ever-constrained mutual interactions, each well-defined and well-understood in itself. But the totality of its effect is also radically disarticulated from such specific conditions – impossible to reduce to simple causal chains. The machine is at once constrictive and generative; at once the site of precise procedure and ambivalent play.

## 2 Theory: Corpus

It is the task of the corpus curator to train the user.[33] Such "training" consists not only in the use of the tools and interfaces to search or access texts but in how to think about the corpus as a distinct kind of object. Curation is Janus-faced. It looks, on the one hand, to individual texts and metadata with the goal of creating versatile digital editions. On the other hand, it seeks to harness the affordances of the corpus as scalable computational object, as a mesh of related, interconnected texts that serves as a proxy for the underlying cultural landscape. This is a perspective that is fundamentally unfamiliar. It has its biases and pitfalls, but also offers unique insights, new spaces for discovery, and serendipitous encounters. How do we balance the twin goals of curating accessible individual texts and navigating the corpus as a collective body of information?

To curate the corpus primarily as corpus – rather than a collection of individual texts – is to attend to questions of scale and modeling as first-order questions: issues that are fundamentally humanistic rather than technical problems to solve. It is in this aspect that the curator becomes a trainer – a guide through the emerging possibilities of the corpus. Of course, like the labor involved in editing a text, much of the task of corpus curation is technical drudgery – encoding texts, correcting errors, gathering metadata, building interfaces. And just as an edition opens up certain avenues of thinking about a text and, in a certain sense, teaches *how* and not just what to read, a corpus, too, provides a template that shapes our thinking, an entry point into a scalable, somewhat disorienting but also exhilarating way of conceptualizing culture. However, both the technology

---

[33] For variations of this general sentiment, I am grateful to Stephen Pentecost and other members of the EarlyPrint team. I founded the EarlyPrint project and served as co-principal investigator on a grant awarded by the ACLS. "Early Print," December 29, 2022, https://earlyprint.org/ (accessed December 29 2022). For reviews of the project, see Lisa Meloncon, "Early Modern Print: Text Mining Early Printed English," *Spenser Review* 46, no. 1 (2016), www.english.cam.ac.uk/spenseronline/review/item/46.1.16/; and Craig A. Berry, "The Lab and the Library: An Introduction to the EarlyPrint Project," *The Spenser Review* 53, no. 2 (2023), https://spenserreview.org/article/id/35/.

and the scale involved in curating and accessing a corpus often seem fundamentally alien to our accustomed ways of encountering texts. It therefore falls to the curator to nudge us, to guide us to look beyond techne to the rhetorical, exploratory, and generative dimensions of the corpus. The encounter with technology – even though it might require some effort – is the easy part. But it also becomes a barrier to the larger, more provocative scholarly purchase of the corpus. Most users are happy to offload to technology the drudgery of what McGann described as the "precritical occupations" of "sorting, assessing, and disseminating" texts.[34] But to see technology as a medium suited to our hermeneutic purposes, as something that can accommodate rhetoric, ambiguity, and serendipity, requires a reorientation that transcends any technical skilling.

In the case of the EarlyPrint team, these questions arose in the process of curating the Early English Books Online – Text Creation Partnership (EEBO-TCP) corpus and building a set of tools around it to facilitate access, exploration, and analysis. There are pragmatic considerations that guide and limit the scope of any such project. These range from general concerns about who the target audience might be for a scholarly curation project to issues of institutional support and technical infrastructure. One persistent point of friction as we curated the corpus was the tension between our own scholarly interests and those of our anticipated audience. Often, we took this ideal user to be a sort of Everyman, some average generalization of "early modern scholar." But, of course, each individual user approaches the corpus differently, bringing unique interests, questions, and, as often, preconceptions about the utility of text at such scale. Many approach the corpus with a pragmatic goal in mind. Some are interested in retrieving and reading single texts – perhaps in modernized spelling or alongside facsimiles, maybe in a pedagogical context engaging with book history. Others might want to retrieve some text or passage or look up some information in the metadata. Others seek more evidence for some already formed or forming hypothesis – perhaps looking for uses of a word or image they are studying. Yet others might approach the corpus looking to utilize its specific affordances as a large collection of texts spread out over the first

[34] McGann, *Radiant Textuality*, 73.

centuries of English print. Perhaps they want to trace the evolution of something over time or find texts that relate to each other in some way.

All of these tasks – especially at the scale of a corpus of this size – require some engineering to make tractable. Under the hood, database tables are optimized, texts indexed into search engines, metadata parsed – networks buzz, hard drives whirr, and circuits crackle metaphorically with the hum of activity. But complex and interesting as these technical challenges might be, in humanistic terms they still broadly occupy the space of "precritical operations" – operations such as information retrieval and search that we take for granted as capabilities of digital systems. It is, of course, impossible to anticipate every possible research question and to accommodate within a set of tools and interfaces designed to serve real-time queries over the web. The corpus has blindnesses, information that is simply missing or, at times, computationally very expensive to track and retrieve.[35] In the next section, I will discuss a set of such operations under the broad category of "search" and argue that they require considerable intervention, both theoretical and algorithmic, and that by relegating them merely to the domain of *techne* we run the risk of overlooking their interpretive dimensions and thus misunderstanding the results they generate.

However, there's another class of more open-ended queries that the corpus lends itself to – open-ended because they rarely produce exhaustive or even definitive results that can be cited as fact. Instead, such queries tend to generate results that are suggestive, partial – the hint of a pattern, the suggestion of an underlying commonality, outlines of a possible trend.

---

[35] For example, a few years ago Claire Bourne asked whether it might be possible to search for manicules and other typographic features in the corpus as part of her research for *Typographies of Performance in Early Modern England* (Oxford: Oxford University Press, 2020). Such features were unfortunately almost never encoded in the EEBO-TCP XML. I myself have wanted to track typeface changes over time and within texts – something not recorded in the EEBO-TCP XML files but definitely possible if one has access to EEBO scans. Others, like a query wanting to detect commonplace markers in plays, might be feasible as a custom project, but is hardly general enough or a common enough query to anticipate in a web interface.

They often lead to further questions rather than answers. Rather than the end-point of empirical evidence to cement an argument, they are often the beginnings of intellectual journeys. They are intensely scalable, but often partial because each individual query seems to present only one strand of a more complex pattern. They are empirical in terms of the underlying bits of texts and information they track, but add up to generative, deformative projections of patterns within the corpus – patterns that, often, can only be seen from the unique vantage point of scale. I will address this broad category of queries that frequently requires further customized analysis and model building with the corpus in the final section under the rubric of "discovery." Such models are thoroughly computational, and intensely scalable, often requiring quite significant technical skill and statistical sophistication. But, perhaps contrary to the hard lines between qualitative and quantitative, close and distant, that have been drawn around the more familiar polemics about computation in the humanities, I shall argue that such models are deeply qualitative and interpretive. I do not mean this in the usual sense of doing distant reading to eventually find one's way back to the familiar terrain of individual texts and passages. Such modeling allows us to glimpse facets of culture that we care about, but that elude our field of view beyond a certain scale.

Very few such queries can be anticipated or actualized in the form of a simple interface or web-based tool. But probing at the corpus from multiple vantage points and multiple perspectives, at multiple scales, is essential to generating the kinds of questions that require scalable modeling. In many ways, such queries are not within the domain of corpus curation – they are too diffused, too complex, too obscure. But, as I have argued, it is the task of the curator to train us to ask questions that need such queries – questions that require us to think about scale and to model deeply nuanced qualitative phenomena in terms of minute, empirically observable building blocks.

## *Scale*

Scale has been one of the key innovations of the digital turn – one of its most alluring promises, as well as one of its most controversial properties. It gestures at previously unattainable perspectives, new horizons of knowledge, and exciting methodological and theoretical innovations. At the same time, it is viewed with suspicion – at best, naïvely imposing borrowed and blunt instruments incommensurable with the nuanced tonalities of interpretation; at worst, a symptom of creeping neoliberalism's gradual encroachment on the intellectual as much as the institutional foundations of the humanities. Under various designations – distant reading, scalable reading, cultural analytics, literary informatics – it has inspired and provoked in equal measure. As the ongoing debates surrounding it indicate, the concept of "scale" remains somewhat unsettled while at once the source of interesting theoretical, not to mention technical innovation. But it is interesting that most of these designations approach the concept of scale when applied to cultural corpora through a set of somewhat reductive oppositions or contradictions. They either emphasize the destabilization of the expectations and hermeneutic processes associated with "reading" by modifying it with an adjective that seems to undo and undermine its fundamental commitments, or, in other cases, they emphasize a quantitative methodology – informatics, analytics – under which the qualitative dimensions of culture seem to be subsumed.

The most notable and theoretically productive among these interventions has been Franco Moretti's formulation of the phrase "distant reading," which signals an implicit and provocative opposition to "close reading." Coined at the height of the canon wars, the term gained notoriety when it was developed as a theoretical formulation of scalable and quantitative approaches to literary history in Moretti's seminal *Graphs, Maps, Trees* (2007). Moretti himself refers to it as a "fatal formula" which was originally meant as a joke, but seems to relish and even embrace the controversy and attention it brought, such as when he is alleged to have urged that we should all "stop reading."[36] Any encounter with Moretti's wide-ranging

---

[36] The claim is often highlighted in popular accounts of Moretti's methodology. See, for example, Kathryn Schulz, "The Mechanic Muse: What Is Distant Reading?," *The New York Times* (June 24, 2011); and Andrea D'Cruz, "Reading Graphs, Maps, and Trees: Timothy Burke Responds to Franco Moretti," *Versobooks.Com* (blog) (accessed July 23, 2022), https://bit.ly/40tAk2S. Moretti has, of course, become a controversial figure since the #metoo movement. For

scholarship, which showcases the astonishing breadth of his own reading, only heightens the irony of such claims and deepens the suspicion that we are witnessing a very specific rhetorical and theoretical reorientation of what is at stake in "reading." Distant "reading," therefore, is both a kind of reading and not-reading. What might have begun as ludic provocation becomes a site for theoretical innovation, its main rhetorical purchase being to interrupt our preconceptions of reading and the kinds of knowledge it produces:

> But within that old territory, a new object of study: instead of concrete, individual works, a trio of artificial constructs – graphs, maps, trees – in which the reality of the text undergoes a process of deliberate reduction and abstraction. 'Distant reading' I have once called this type of approach; where distance is however not an obstacle but *a specific form of knowledge*: fewer elements, hence a sharper sense of their overall interconnection. Shapes, relations, structures. Forms. Models.[37]

The innovation Moretti proposes, it turns out, is fundamentally one of perspective achieved through transformations applied to the text: "processes of deliberate reduction and abstraction" that McGann and Samuels' deformative reading practices exemplified for us and that, in turn, go back to core critical notions of defamiliarization as a fundamental characteristic of literary language. But Moretti's transformative intervention does not stop at deformance. Whereas deformative reading, like much formalist, structuralist, and poststructuralist reading, is invested in disrupting hermeneutic frameworks to open up the text to the other kinds of ambiguity, play, and

a call for rethinking his position in the academy, a good starting point is Lauren F. Klein, "Distant Reading After Moretti," *Arcade: The Humanities in the World* (January 29, 2018), https://shc.stanford.edu/arcade/interventions/distant-reading-after-moretti.

[37] Franco Moretti, *Graphs, Maps, Trees: Abstract Models for Literary History* (Verso, 2007), 1 (emphasis original).

polyvalence, distant reading emerges from such abstractive transformation in a countermove that imposes a kind of uniformity – the imposition of shared patterns: "Shapes, relations, structures. Forms. Models." Moretti's choice of terminology is significant. From the keywords structuring his book – graphs, maps, trees – to this final dyad – "Forms. Models" – his terms resonate between the familiar patterns and structures of literary reading and those of quantitative, computational analysis. They perform the transformation of one into the other.

Indeed, many other scholars have sought to find similar continuities with traditional modes of humanistic reading, while at once pointing to the radical hermeneutic disruption that scale accomplishes. Ted Underwood, for example, has lamented the ways in which the ideas of distance and scale have been tied to narrow notions of a "digital turn." Instead, he has argued that scale has a long prehistory from nineteenth-century "old historicism" to the scholars such as Raymond Williams and Janice Radway, who have sought to see the development of literary and cultural history in terms of the unfolding of large-scale theoretical models.[38] Elsewhere, Underwood and James English have traced a more expansive "crisis of largeness" wherein a defining turn from New Critical preoccupations with form and the isolated mechanics of single textual artifacts gives way to a broad interest in historicism.[39] In fact, English and Underwood go even further to give an account of the historical arc of literary scholarship "as essentially a drama of competing scales" that has had an inherent bias toward scale.[40] Andrew Piper has sought to place the investments in scale in a similar relationship of continuity with previous modes of criticism. He takes as his prototype the impossibly vast scholarly cultural landscape that Eric Auerbach's *Mimesis* sought to map and asks, rhetorically, "Who could ever claim to possess such erudition?" Auerbach's ambitious approach, despite the daunting erudition

[38] Ted Underwood, "A Genealogy of Distant Reading," *Digital Humanities Quarterly* 11, no. 2 (2017): 5, www.digitalhumanities.org/dhq/vol/11/2/000317/000317.html.

[39] James F. English and Ted Underwood, "Shifting Scales Between Literature and Social Science," *Modern Language Quarterly* 77, no. 3 (2016): 279.

[40] English and Underwood, "Shifting Scales," 278.

he brings to the task, can only paper over a central crisis, an "epistemological tragedy" that lies at the heart of literary criticism: "*Mimesis* dramatized, perhaps more than any other work in the field before or since, the metonymical crisis that lay at the core of literary criticism, an incommensurable relationship between part and whole."[41] This incommensurability returns as tragedy or blindness in many discussions of scale. Scale itself, therefore, is not alien to the goals and aspirations of literary scholarship. In fact, it is quite the opposite. It represents the very horizon to which literary criticism aspires: "The literary critic, stationed at a distance, captured the inaccessibility of the cultural whole to which his knowledge aspired."[42] But, alas, limited as we are in the kinds and quantities of things we can attend to, scale remains an ever-receding horizon, one which we can only gesture at and extrapolate from a necessarily limited sample.

Distance, therefore, as perspective – a mode of knowledge that is not fundamentally alien to the humanities. Scale, according to this account, has been an ever-present concern within the broad arc of cultural criticism. The technological infrastructure of modern computation certainly facilitates it, but is not a precondition of thinking about or theorizing scale. Underwood asserts "I want to emphasize that distant reading is not a new trend, defined by digital technology or by contemporary obsession with the word *data* ... [T]he central practice that distinguishes distant reading from other forms of literary criticism is not at bottom a technology."[43] While the general claim rings true, one might point out that it is with the availability of computational tools and techniques – storage, processing power, algorithms – that such scalable approaches have come to the fore. In other words, the significant, even determining, role played by computation cannot be overlooked in any account of the (re)emergence of scale as a critical concern. Thus, a critique of scale – regardless of conceptual continuity – as manifested in computational and quantitative practices remains necessary. Quite apart from the theoretical continuity that scholars such as Underwood and Piper have argued for so convincingly, the computational practices involved in corpus-level analysis

---

[41] Andrew Piper, *Enumerations: Data and Literary Study*, First edition (Chicago: University of Chicago Press, 2018), 7.

[42] Piper, *Enumerations*, 7.   [43] Underwood, "A Genealogy," 5.

need to be amenable to the demands of literary analysis. As we move from the kind of play and polymorphism that the individual text facilitates to scalable corpus-level analysis, we must be able to accommodate within quantitative and computational models the kind of intertextuality and abstraction we have claimed for distant reading practices.

## *Model*

The move from text to corpus is a deeply disorienting one. However, the change in perspective is not the main axis of unfamiliarity here. We are – as Underwood and Piper, along with many other scholars, have pointed out – used to thinking at scale, only in a different mode. Extrapolating patterns from the particular to the general is one of the characteristic tasks of literary and cultural criticism. We move from closely observed, nuanced engagements with texts to large-scale patterns: trends, structures, formations, trajectories of change. Every theoretical paradigm offers ways of thinking about the relationship of the particular to the general, of mapping relationships, tracing pathways of influence, structures of causality and change. From structure to field, from topologies of rhizomes to actor-networks – critical theory abounds in such "models" designed to scale up our thinking. At times such theoretical models come quite close to conceptualizing culture as a complex information-processing system. The difficulty is not in the concept of extrapolating general patterns from particular observations, but in the different ways literary theoretical and quantitative models represent information and the assumptions they make. We should not presume any simple equivalence or continuity between the qualitative theoretical models we are used to and the kind of scalable quantitative modeling that computation lends itself to. There are, as Moretti and many others have pointed out, striking homologies and shared structures, perhaps even closely mirrored underlying premises and goals. These can occasion fruitful points of departure for debate and theorization. But there are significant differences as well. Network graphs are not alive to the intricacies of the rhizome, nor does the most complex simulation accommodate all nuances of the field of cultural production. But computational models have their own affordances, too – their own modes of transforming information that would be opaque to us if we insisted merely on treating them as imperfect, stunted analogs of qualitative ways of mapping and modeling. We need to attend to the specificity of the quantitative paradigm – its strengths as well as its blind spots – if we are to engage with models as more than structuring metaphors and to harness them for the purposes of literary reading and analysis.

While discussions of scale have mostly emphasized the role of modeling as providing a transformed perspective, most humanistic objections about modeling seem to be grounded in a deeper set of reservations. Quantitative models, it is alleged, are unable to accommodate the nuances of humanistic reading and analysis on at least two fronts: complexity and ambiguity. The notion that models simplify the complex intersection and interplay that characterizes theoretical paradigms is an often repeated allegation. And it is substantially true. Richard So summarizes this suspicion that quantitative modeling, ipso facto, is incapable of accommodating humanistic complexity: "Literary scholars have long cast a suspicious and critical gaze toward modeling, which strikes them as offensively simpleminded and naive: models run counter to the deep and intensive reading that literary critics take pride in, the exposing of nuance and singularity in texts, writers, and human beings."[44] Indeed, as in Moretti's account of modeling as "a process of deliberate reduction and abstraction," models are often described in terms of "helpful simplification."[45] Models, therefore, are theoretical representations that actively seek to ignore – or, at least, to drastically reduce – complexity to throw certain features into relief: "Modeling is the process of formalizing our framework for interpreting the world around us by abstracting from a reality that is otherwise too complex to understand."[46] Such a model does not strive to meet the challenge of complexity thought of as granularity and detail. Its notion of complexity is different. It reveals complexity in terms of connections, similarities, shared patterns – in other words, in terms of intertextuality. It flattens the intratextual to heighten our sense of the intertextual.

---

[44] Richard Jean So, "All Models Are Wrong," *PMLA* 132, no. 3 (2017): 668.
[45] Moretti, *Graphs, Maps, Trees*, 1; and W. James Bradley and Kurt Schaefer, *The Uses and Misuses of Data and Models: The Mathematization of the Human Sciences* (Thousand Oaks, CA: SAGE Publications, 1998), 23.
[46] Bradley and Schaefer, *The Uses and Misuses*, 23.

Others have suggested that models are growing increasingly adept at accommodating, rather than flattening or eliminating, complexity. More features or variables, it is assumed, result in models that overcome any objection about imposing a forced simplicity and approach a degree of complexity that is an ever closer approximation of "reality."[47] However, much of this capacity to handle nuance has been driven by fundamental conceptual recalibrations of how we might think about complex, uncertain, and indeterminate phenomena. As scholars such as English and Underwood have emphasized, "forms of epistemological reflection" or conceptual interventions have been the driving factor of such change, even though increased computational power has facilitated their implementation.[48] In fact, I would broaden the horizon of this development to suggest that thinking about unpredictable, indeterminate phenomena is one of the cornerstones of twentieth-century science and its ongoing developments. From quantum mechanics to information theory, various fields have made advancements in thinking about phenomena that cannot be reduced to exactly repeatable chains of causality – phenomena that are inherently stochastic, indeterminate, and emergent. When McGann, as we saw in the previous section, gravitates toward the notion of "quantum criticism," its fundamentally indeterminate "stochastic" nature is what he repeatedly cites as the correlate of humanistic notions of polyvalence and ambiguity.

From the virtues of simplicity that throw patterns of intertextuality into relief, to claims of growing complexity that can accommodate ambiguity, both the understanding and utility of models have evolved over time. However, certain strands of skepticism persist. Most often, this takes the form of a fundamental, axiomatically held conviction that "human and literary phenomena are irreducible to numbers."[49] Such convictions are widely

---

[47] Notice, for example, the reporting of the number of parameters that accompany the release of large language models (LLMs) such as GPT or BERT – numbers which are already in the hundreds of billions and promising (or perhaps threatening) to reach the trillions quite soon.

[48] English and Underwood, "Shifting Scales," 286.

[49] Nan Z. Da, "The Computational Case against Computational Literary Studies," *Critical Inquiry* 45, no. 3 (2019): 604.

held, even if rarely articulated as methodically as Nan Z. Da does in her much-discussed paper, wherein she summarizes her objections to quantitative and computational work thus: "In a nutshell the problem with computational literary analysis as it stands is that what is robust is obvious (in the empirical sense) and what is not obvious is not robust, a situation not easily overcome given the nature of literary data and the nature of statistical inquiry."[50] It is not my purpose here to take issue with Da's paper or the critiques of particular digital projects she puts forward. There have been several venues that have facilitated that discussion.[51] But the debate she initiates about the nature of literary "complexity" and whether quantitative methods are fundamentally incommensurable with it serves as a reminder of widespread skepticism in the field. Unfortunately, much of this discussion happens in a tone of antagonism, each side feeling that their most foundational commitments are under attack. Complexity and ambiguity are not the sole domain of hermeneutics, we are reminded. On the other hand, quantitative methodologies are charged with espousing a shallow, dogmatic empiricism.

Ultimately, computational methodologies will need to demonstrate their utility. But some reconsideration of what such demonstration might consist of is essential. As long as we hold to the notion that there is a fundamental incommensurability between quantification and the modeling of ambiguity, and that any approach that begins with the observation of empirical facts about texts is destined to get stuck within limited notions of proof, testability, and perfect repeatability, we will restrict such methods to a small

---

[50] Da, "The Computational Case," 601.

[51] See, for example, Fotis Jannidis, "On the Perceived Complexity of Literature. a Response to Nan Z. Da," *Journal of Cultural Analytics* 5, no. 1 (2020), https://doi.org/10.22148/001c.11829; Ted Underwood, "The Theoretical Divide Driving Debates about Computation," *Critical Inquiry* 46, no. 4 (2020): 900–12, https://doi.org/10.1086/709229; Leif Weatherby, "Prolegomena to a Theory of Data: On the Most Recent Confrontation of Data and Literature," *Critical Inquiry* 46, no. 4 (2020): 891–9, https://doi.org/10.1086/709228; and Da's own response to the debate in "On EDA, Complexity, and Redundancy: A Response to Underwood and Weatherby," *Critical Inquiry* 46, no. 4 (2020): 913–24, https://doi.org/10.1086/709230.

subdomain of problems. To be sure, there are problems within literary studies that can be reduced to the parameters of a yes/no formulation of proof. At times, these problems are interesting and can benefit significantly from computational interventions – stylometrical analysis, for example, when used to probe issues of authorship. But, by and large, this constitutes a limited range of problems. Other problems, especially those dealing with the long arc of literary history – evolutions of style, genre, patterns of publishing – also benefit from "empirical" analysis, but they often fail to assuage the objections of skeptics who hold such analysis as either working with a very reductive set of features or merely pushing into the domain of proof and statistical testing of what was "obvious" all along.

This dogmatism about quantification often arises from a fundamentally flawed notion of statistics and information theory and the ways these disciplines have radically reshaped our ability to model ambiguous, amorphous phenomena and incredibly complex chains of causality. We need to remind ourselves that a statistical approach itself does not rule out the possibility of accommodating ambiguity. Statistics would not be required in a world of perfectly predictable precision. In fact, one might say that statistics exists because we need to model a world that is not precise, predictable, or computable in any reductive sense – a world that we can only describe in terms of partial, fragmented observations and must speak of in terms of chance, probability, tendencies, likelihood, degrees of belief. To think about a corpus as a fundamentally scalable computational object that lends itself to quantitative modeling is to learn to recognize a continuity – rather than a radical break – between the humanistic engagement with details and their agglomerative, accumulated patterns that escape our localized modes of attention. As custodian of both text and archive, of edition and corpus, it is the task of the curator to facilitate such continuity. The corpus, insofar as it can model culture as a deeply stochastic field of multiple, interlinked processes often irreducible to precise chains of causality, opens up ways of thinking about the kinds of deformance, play, and generative critique that literary scholars have come to value in the digital edition.

### *Case Study: EEBO-TCP*

The Early English Books Online – Text Creation Partnership (EEBO-TCP) corpus has been at the center of debates about the role of digitization in mediating access, on the one hand, and allowing scalable abstraction, modeling, and quantitative analysis, on the other.[52] Created by a decades-long transcription project, the EEBO-TCP corpus aimed to have a hand-transcribed copy of at least one edition of every book printed in English or in England, Scotland, or Wales before 1700. These transcriptions were created from the page scans of volumes from Early English Books Online (EEBO), a proprietary database of scans of what were originally images of pages from books listed in *A Short-Title Catalogue* (STC) and its sequel, compiled by Donald Wing.[53] The transcriptions made the original EEBO corpus of image scans searchable as full texts and were released into the public domain in two phases.[54] The corpus comprises TEI encoded XML files totaling about 1.7 billion tokens or words representing the history of printed English up to 1700. The corpus derives its metadata from the *English Short Title Catalogue*, which in turn extracts the data mostly from the encoding of title pages with and STC/Wing data.[55] EEBO-TCP's massive impact on pedagogy and research is undeniable: it has become an integral part of everyday scholarship as a reference corpus. Especially as a free, searchable corpus available in the public domain, EEBO-TCP has

---

[52] "Early English Books Online – Text Creation Partnership," https://bit.ly/4h3x4CG, accessed June 8, 2024. For a curated version of the corpus, see "Early Print." Unless otherwise mentioned, I will draw my data from EarlyPrint.

[53] Alfred W. Pollard, G.R. Redgrave, et al., *A Short-Title Catalogue of Books Printed in England, Scotland, & Ireland and of English Books Printed Abroad, 1475–1640*, 2nd ed. (London: The Bibliographical Society, 1976); and Donald Goddard Wing et al., *Short-Title Catalogue of Books Printed in England, Scotland, Ireland, Wales, and British America, and of English Books Printed in Other Countries, 1641–1700*, 2nd ed. (New York: Modern Language Association of America, 1994).

[54] Phase 1 of the EEBO-TCP corpus, comprising about 25,000 volumes, was released into the public domain on January 1, 2015 with phase II, comprising a further 45,000 volumes, released on August 1, 2020.

[55] "English Short Title Catalogue," http://estc.bl.uk/ (accessed December 28, 2017).

done wonders in increasing access to key texts and resources to the many institutions and individuals outside the select few (mostly Western) universities that could afford the quite hefty subscription fee to license EEBO from ProQuest.

But the impact of the corpus is not limited to facilitating access alone. As a digitally encoded, computationally tractable corpus, EEBO-TCP has opened up new avenues of research and new modes of thinking about and exploring early modern print culture and history. As the metadata accompanying the corpus has continued to improve, it has fostered a renewed interest in book-historical scholarship, while the scale of the corpus has been leveraged for heavily quantitative and computational scholarship exploring the stylistic and material dimensions of literary and print culture. Perhaps somewhat surprisingly, given that computational text analysis has often been suspected or accused of promoting a kind of ahistorical and quantitative abstraction that sees texts as isolated constructs stripped of material and cultural specificity, much of the heavily computational work that has been done on EEBO-TCP, as well as other digital projects exploring subdomains of early modern print culture, has paid attention to materiality and the concrete historical processes of textual transmission and social and institutional organizations within which early modern texts were produced and circulated. For example, scholars have used computational techniques to study the circulation and reuse of woodcuts in broadside ballads, the networks of patronage within which books were produced, the structures of theatrical affiliation and the collaborations they engendered using scans and metadata collected through EEBO-TCP and through projects such as the English Broadside Ballad Archive (EBBA), Six Degrees of Francis Bacon, and the Database of Early English Playbooks (DEEP).[56] Moreover, EEBO scans and EEBO-TCP encodings have been used to trace anonymous printers, poetic style, and archaism.[57]

---

[56] Patricia Fumerton, dir. "UCSB English Broadside Ballad Archive," https://ebba.english.ucsb.edu/; "Six Degrees of Francis Bacon," www.sixdegreesoffrancisbacon.com/ (accessed June 5, 2023); and Zachary Lesser and Alan Farmer, ed., "DEEP: Database of Early English Playbooks," http://deep.sas.upenn.edu/.

[57] Anupam Basu, Jonathan Hope, and Michael Witmore, "Networks and Communities in the Early Modern Theatre," in *Community-Making in Early*

However, while there is an increasing recognition of such possibilities, a deep note of unease persists about accommodating the computational aspects of EEBO into the domain of humanities scholarship. In recent years, there have been several attempts at documenting the history and scope of EEBO-TCP that trace the complex material, institutional, and scholarly genealogy of the corpus and its many transformations.[58] Such histories are almost unfailingly laudatory of the scale of the project and the ways it has facilitated access, and sensitive to the instabilities of the many mediating technologies and formats that have led to the current versions of EEBO and EEBO-TCP. But, with the notable exception of Michael Gavin's rousing account, most of these histories register not only a kind of unease but what

---

*Stuart Theatres: Stage and Audience*, ed. Roger Sell and Anthony Johnson (Farnham, England: 2014); Christopher N. Warren, Daniel Shore, Jessica Otis, et al., "Six Degrees of Francis Bacon: A Statistical Method for Reconstructing Large Historical Social Networks," *Digital Humanities Quarterly* 10, no. 3 (2016); Carl G. Stahmer, "Digital Analytical Bibliography: Ballad Sheet Forensics, Preservation, and the Digital Archive," *Huntington Library Quarterly* 79, no. 2 (2016): 263–78; Warren et al., "Damaged Type and *Areopagitica*'s Clandestine Printers," *Milton Studies* 62, no. 1 (2020): 1–47; Anupam Basu and Joseph Loewenstein, "Spenser's Spell: Archaism and Historical Stylometrics," *Spenser Studies* 33 (2019): 63–102; John R. Ladd, "Imaginative Networks: Tracing Connections Among Early Modern Book Dedications," *Journal of Cultural Analytics* 6, no. 1 (2021); and James Lee, Blaine Greteman, Jason Lee, et al., "Linked Reading: Digital Historicism and Early Modern Discourses of Race around Shakespeare's Othello," *Journal of Cultural Analytics* 3, no. 1 (2018).

[58] Stephen Tabor, "ESTC and the Bibliographical Community," *The Library: The Transactions of the Bibliographical Society* 8, no. 4 (2007): 367–86; Ian Gadd, "The Use and Misuse of Early English Books Online," *Literature Compass* 6, no. 3 (2009): 680–92; Bonnie Mak, "Archaeology of a Digitization," *Journal of the Association for Information Science and Technology* 65, no. 8 (2014): 1515–26; Kathryn Sutherland and Marilyn Deegan, *Transferred Illusions: Digital Technology and the Forms of Print* (London: Routledge, 2016); Michael Gavin, "How To Think About EEBO," *Textual Cultures* 11, no. 1–2 (2017): 70–105; Peter C. Herman, "EEBO and Me: An Autobiographical Response to Michael Gavin, 'How to Think About EEBO,'" *Textual Cultures* 13, no. 1 (2020): 207–17.

might be described as distrust when it comes to thinking of the digital and specifically scalable affordances of the corpus. In many ways, this skepticism mirrors our seeming difficulty in negotiating the digital text as also a computational one and the kinds of antagonism that structure many responses to scale and model. Much of the skepticism and unease about the digital format arises from an inability to look beyond the problem of access as the final frontier of digitization. In other words, it is assumed that the primary – if not the only – reason one would take the trouble of digitizing something – either as scans or as encodings (two very different forms, with drastically different affordances that are often collapsed under the umbrella term "digital") – would be to create a reasonable proxy of an underlying text for reading.

Most critiques, therefore, are directed to sites of failure in approaching this purported goal of digital surrogacy. The points such arguments make are often quite valid in themselves, but they also often speak of the digital text as a somewhat flattened and imperfect proxy of the text it represents; or, perhaps even worse, they worry that the users of such corpora will naïvely mistake the digital facsimile for the text itself. This leads to a curious set of concerns about how the digital medium threatens to transfix us in a technological rendering of Plato's cave, enchanted by shadows and mistaking them for the reality that would be apparent to us if only we cared to turn around. But why is the digital form particularly susceptible to such illusion? Why not acknowledge, as decades of textual theory has taught us, that, as we dig down through the layers of mediation that a text undergoes, questions of textual instability do not disappear once we hit the material text? The mediation that digitization introduces is only one step in a long chain of always already mediated textual transmission. Curiously, as mentioned earlier, much of this scholarship is acutely alive to the instabilities of text and the interventions that happen as such texts are translated between media. So, it is fair to ask, what is it about scale and digitization that makes such insightful scholars worry in particular about the fragility of text and about an uncritical acceptance of the evidence of shadows? Is it the supposed ephemerality of the medium? Is it the unrestricted access beyond the select realm of specialists? Is it scale? Is it quantification?

Stephen Tabor's observations about young people "lured" in by the razzle-dazzle and easy availability of scans who therefore ignore the complexity and diversity of the underlying material texts and print culture is representative of this tone of lament:

> An increasingly common trend, I am sorry to report, is that more and more people do not want ESTC at all – they want ECCO or EEBO. The younger generation of scholars in particular, lured by full-text images and ransacking the Web for illustrations for their books and articles, are using these utilities as de facto bibliographic databases. They find that the stripped-down records and simplified indexes are good enough for their purposes.[59]

Similar notes are sounded by Ian Gadd, who warns against the "misuse" of EEBO while maintaining that his goal is "not to accuse EEBO of misrepresenting what it contains," but "both students and scholars" are likely to fall into the errors of assuming, first, that EEBO is a complete account of the printed textual record and, second, that the particular image-set contained in EEBO (and hence encoded in EEBO-TCP) represents, somehow, the edition represented in the ESTC bibliographical record rather than a particular witness often collected under severe material and time constraints: "Ironically, the unprecedented and apparently unfettered access to early printed books that EEBO provides appears to have coincided with a period when decreasing numbers of students and scholars know how to describe or interpret bibliographically those same books. The rare book room has been thrown open just as the rare book librarians have gone home."[60] These are, to be sure, valid concerns to point out. They are, however, issues about the state of early modern scholarship and pedagogy more broadly, rather than about EEBO itself. Gadd admits that EEBO – or

---

[59] Tabor, "ESTC and the Bibliographical Community," 368. On the question of "good enough" as a qualifying category for the digital corpus, see Rowe, "Living with Digital Incunables."

[60] Gadd, "The Use and Misuse," 682.

EEBO-TCP, for that matter – do not misrepresent any aspect of their corpus, and what he is emphasizing is more the possible danger of misrecognition. What is included, what is not, how it has been processed, discrepancies between the source of the scans and the metadata where they exist, even error rates and missing images, etcetera, can all be easily looked up, computed, and cross-checked. The caveats, therefore, are about the supposed ignorance of users on the simplest aspects of this vital scholarly resource rather than the resource itself. Similarly egregious errors would have been possible to commit if one did not know how to use the catalog or finding aids of a research library or did not think about the relationship of a particular witness of a text at a single library as opposed to the edition or in relation to other extant witnesses.

But such complaints continue to be made as if they are observations about some fundamental aspect of the digital medium. Diana Kichuk, for example, warns of the dangers of the "digital veil" which requires a "suspension of disbelief": "The EEBO image is virtual. Although it manifests itself as a real object, it lacks the physicality of its microfilm or print predecessors."[61] How the materiality of microfilm is of more consequence than that of the hardware and technology required to access EEBO remains unclear.[62] However, even as she repeatedly reminds us that the value of EEBO and EEBO-TCP "cannot be understated," she belabors what must surely seem, at least to any scholarly audience, an obvious point: that the digital facsimile doesn't replace the book, let alone any notion of the "original" book. The versions in EEBO, she reminds us, are "certainly not identical copies of the one pulled from the printing press, bound, and read when first published." Does anyone think they are? At best, this is a point about pedagogy – that we need to familiarize students better with the basic elements of book history, and perhaps also remind them that even the "originals" in the stacks of the Bodleian, the Folger, or the Huntington are "not identical copies of the one pulled from the printing press, bound, and

---

[61] Diana Kichuk, "Metamorphosis: Remediation in Early English Books Online (EEBO)," *Literary and Linguistic Computing* 22, no. 3 (2007): 296.

[62] And, as noted in the first section, scholars such as Kirschenbaum have elaborated on the very complex materialities that underlie the digital medium.

read when first published." But this oversimplistic account of the errors that EEBO might lead us to is not really a lesson on book history – it is a warning about the seductions of the digital:

> Like the modern connoisseur of Renaissance paintings who prefers the darkened and faded colors created by time and environmental assaults rather than the vividly colored restoration, the student and scholar of Early English books runs the risk of revering the digital image in all its surrogate glory, and preferring it to the print book it is replicating.[63]

The supposed erasure of the material foundations of the archive, to the extent that we stop caring about the books underlying the scans and transcriptions, is an incessant motif in the scholarship on EEBO. And somehow, more than any previous remediation, as Bonnie Mak alleges, EEBO encourages us to overlook the materiality of the corpus.[64]

This pervasive fear of erasure, of having materiality disappear from our frame of reference, bears some contemplation – especially as curators of the vast corpus that apparently precipitates this fear. As noted earlier, it is rooted in a fundamental misrecognition of the digital form as somehow a mere proxy, a necessarily imperfect and therefore deceptive shadow on the wall. As Sutherland and Deegan put it, "EEBO is still essentially a means to access an old medium, the printed book." And, because it is mere shadow, we never pause to ask what the medium does well in itself; we only ponder what it threatens: "Then, again, how long will it be before students and scholars forget that the facsimile texts assembled in EEBO were once books with paper, board and leather bindings?"[65] Even when such scholars celebrate the abstraction enabled by EEBO, it is rooted in the materiality or the potential materiality of the hard copy or downloadable file. Taking issue with Gavin's description of EEBO-TCP as a corpus that encourages a fundamentally interconnected, comparative view of texts, Peter Herman accuses him of "techno-utopianism" and suggests that, instead of greater

---

[63] Kichuk, "Metamorphosis," 302.  [64] Mak, "Archaeology of a Digitization," 1519.
[65] Sutherland and Deegan, *Transferred Illusions*, 90.

abstraction, EEBO and EEBO-TCP have allowed him "greater concreteness."[66] This concreteness, he suggests, comes in the form of search, the ability to quickly download the files, and, finally, the fact that "you can do all of this from your desktop at home." He even mentions, as a measure of added convenience compared to microfilm readers, the fact that it is no longer necessary to scroll, focus, or "bring rolls of dimes" to make copies.[67] Such articulations, when they are not warning us of the coming cultural amnesia about the fact that scans were once books, have a genuine note of excitement about EEBO, as when Herman rather joyfully recounts his personal experience of a transformative scholarly technology: "I can't exaggerate how EEBO has changed my life."[68]

However, such accounts of EEBO's affordances steadfastly refuse to see EEBO and EEBO-TCP as more than shortcuts for saving a trip to the library, taking on an admonishing tone we usually reserve for undergrads who never visit the stacks and instead rely too heavily on Google. They fall woefully short of any conceptualization of digital, let alone computational affordances, or any serious consideration of scale and model as modes of abstraction and thinking intertextuality.[69] Gavin, whose work

[66] Herman, "EEBO and Me," 208.  [67] Herman, "EEBO and Me," 210.
[68] Herman, "EEBO and Me," 210.
[69] As a secondary note that I worry might distract from our focus on the scalable dimensions of the corpus, it might be useful to ask to what extent such anxieties about the wide availability of EEBO and the consequent erosion of scholarly rigor are rooted in implicit hierarchies of academic elitism and the politics of access. Herman notes, as one possible serious objection to EEBO-TCP, the fact that transcriptions were performed by coders in "India, . . . China, Nicaragua, Vietnam, and of course, Philippines" (215). He remarks that "these are not countries known for high wages and worker benefits. EEBO-TCP, in other words, is made possible by the same global economy that grants the first world cheap clothing and affordable electronics." While this is an important caveat to sound and certainly worth investigating, it is rather presumptuous to group all knowledge economies within those countries together. Conversely, one should remember that this resulted in a public domain resource rather than a closely guarded and prohibitively costly proprietary one that will benefit institutions in those and other countries in perpetuity.

on EEBO formed the foundation of the quantitative analysis he uses in his book *Literary Mathematics*, expresses some frustration at these repeated caveats about EEBO and EEBO-TCP and suggests that it expresses something of a generational divide rather than a substantive scholarly argument: "Kids today ... with their Snapchat, their Tinder, and their EEBO!"[70] His exasperation is perhaps understandable. After all, even though he gives nuanced and detailed accounts of both the bibliographical history of EEBO and the technologies of its transmission, he is deeply interested in leveraging the quantitative affordances of EEBO-TCP and argues that books, regardless of physical or digital format, are "abstract objects with representable attributes." Herman's essay, which actually forms a response to Gavin's theorization but completely fails to acknowledge the central points of Gavin's argument, shows that the conceptual divide remains quite large.

However, as curators and scholars invested in both access and scale, we need to contend with such reservations about the corpus and ask how we might facilitate better engagement with what often feels so fundamentally alien. Curators, I have suggested, often need to guide users on how to approach the corpus. A curator's goal is to create texts that are as accurate and accessible as possible, but also texts that lend themselves to scalable search, abstraction, and exploration. These two facets are inextricably interlinked. Each interpretive decision is constrained by what is computationally tractable, and each engineering decision must respond to what is useful in a humanistic context. Processes that seem to be "natural" affordances of the digital medium, such as text and metadata search or something as simple as the retrieval and rendering of individual texts, often encode quintessentially interpretive assumptions. If there is a "digital veil" whose enchantment we should be wary of, it is the assumed simplicity or objectivity of opaque technical processes. From cleaning up metadata to ranking search results to extracting trends or patterns – every aspect of the corpus that we might assume to not require particular critical engagement in actuality requires us to deal with fundamentally stochastic and

---

[70] Michael Gavin, *Literary Mathematics: Quantitative Theory for Textual Studies* (Standford, CA: Stanford University Press, 2022); and "How To Think About EEBO," 75.

uncertain processes, processes that encode critical assumptions about salience, similarity, or likelihood. On the other hand, scalable processes that use sophisticated quantitative modeling that might seem as if they are unaccommodating of any ambiguity, functioning merely within the domains of testing and proof, can serve as sites for generative, open-ended exploration and play – as massively scalable deformative projections of the corpus.

In the following sections, I will consider two sets of computational explorations of the corpus: the first might be more familiar to most Shakespearean scholars who use search interfaces to corpora like EEBO: a set of information retrieval or "search" techniques that we might think of as rather mundane computational forms of "looking up" objective data. Secondly, I'll look at some more abstract ways of computationally transforming and modeling patterns in the corpus. These experiments might seem technically more elaborate, but I shall argue that they go beyond "mere" search and align closely with the ways in which literary scholars think about textual culture. Both ends of this spectrum of scalable approaches to the corpus, I shall suggest, defy common expectations of objectivity or the usual boundaries we are accustomed to drawing between quantitative and qualitative, techne and episteme, proof and persuasion.

## 3 Praxis: Search

Search is ubiquitous. As Google's ever-present search bar, or Siri and Alexa's disembodied, dispassionate, yet comforting voices, ceaselessly remind us, search is increasingly our point of access to the world, as it were. The deceptive simplicity of these interfaces, designed to always lurk in the background, nonintrusive and almost invisible, erases the complexity of search as a set of techniques for information retrieval and encourages us to think of it merely as a transparent, transactional "finding tool." The occasional "advanced" tab or settings menu might open up glimpses into the implicit assumptions, priorities, and decisions that mediate our access to information. Still, even such encounters with search-as-techne are shrouded behind layers of often proprietary algorithmic opacity. Consider, for example, the mystique and secrecy attached to the PageRank algorithm, the "secret sauce" that propelled Google's domination of search.[71] It uses a complex set of metrics – inbound and outbound links, clicks, popularity, etcetera – to deduce the importance or rank of a page for a given topic. But almost as important as the technical innovations of the algorithm is Google's other innovation: the dramatically simplified search interface, deliberately sparse and unburdened with the traces of the massive engines churning underneath, not only the logical machinery of interface and algorithm but the very material engines of datacenters and the infrastructures that allow the dissemination of information. It is designed to facilitate our contact with technology, to make it seem a welcoming, nonthreatening, almost whimsical space. The only other things of note on the page apart from the functional "search" button are the fun doodles that are already part of cultural lore and a button that randomly switches to options such as "I'm feeling lucky," "I'm feeling artistic," "I'm feeling trendy." It is a place, the design seems to suggest, where one might hang out and make fanciful deep dives into odd rabbit holes of curiosity and discovery. It is an interface designed precisely to distract us from our encounter with technology even as it facilitates it. We are not meant to think about what exactly goes in the secret sauce or, at times, even about what kind of result we want to retrieve – we type it in and let Google figure out what is best. The layers of algorithms and personalized data use a combination of techniques – some less palatable than others – to retrieve and rank pages. They make assumptions about what is more popular, probable, normal, important, significant, authoritative, etcetera. They combine these with all the alarming things Google either knows or can deduce about our habits, preferences, histories, demographic and economic status, geographic locations, contacts, etcetera. Finally, at the end of this long, long chain of mediations that take microseconds, Google serves up a clean, hierarchically organized set of results. Both the underlying assumptions about highly qualitative categories and the technical machinations by which they are arrived at are conveniently hidden

---

[71] Amy N. Langville and Carl D. Meyer, *Google's PageRank and Beyond: The Science of Search Engine Rankings* (Princeton, NJ: Princeton University Press, 2006); and Anna Crowley Redding, *Google It: A History of Google* (New York: Feiwel & Friends, 2018).

away behind the wholesome, minimalist interface that projects simplicity and whimsy.

This technological sleight of hand is not limited to Google. Nor is Google uniquely sinister. The point, in fact, is about our relationship with technology – the fact that we so comfortably hand off to an opaque technological black box, one of our primary modes of access to information, bears some consideration. Several recent studies have sought to put forward critiques of technology that situate algorithmic culture as a mediator of socioeconomic power structures.[72] However, while such studies offer crucial insights into a rapidly shifting landscape of technology that is overtly invested in global data capitalism, most of our day-to-day encounters with technology in the course of scholarly practice remain largely instrumental. As more and more research, and even ordinary reading, functions within massive digitized and interlinked archives and search, as a broad set of technologies, mediates our very access to them, critical engagement with this supposed instrumental dimension becomes ever more crucial. Rather than being a transparent or neutral instrument of access, search increasingly modulates what we read, how we read, and how we think about reading – it is not just a passive tool for retrieving information but an active mediator in the attention economy. It imposes particular constraints on the forms that readerly attention can take and enhances the scale at which such attention can operate. Understandably, when faced with the scale and complexity that drives today's search paradigms, literary scholars might be inclined to throw in the towel and just trust the veracity of these tools as "finding aids" so long as they do a reasonably good job. To do so, however, is doubly problematic. Not only do we give up technical agency – the ability to exploit the capabilities of the tool as best as possible – but we surrender crucial critical agency as well and risk falling into the illusion that Google's

---

[72] See, for example, Safiya Umoja Noble, *Algorithms of Oppression: How Search Engines Reinforce Racism* (New York: NYU Press, 2018); Catherine D'Ignazio and Lauren F. Klein, *Data Feminism* (Cambridge, MA: MIT Press, 2020); and Mark Graham and Martin Dittus, *Geographies of Digital Exclusion: Data and Inequality* (London: Pluto Press, 2022).

sparse homepage so carefully tries to create for us: the notion that somehow search is "objective."

This is often how we treat search – as if it were an exact, unambiguous operation of precisely coded instructions that are translated into a determinate series of operations to retrieve results that constitute a perfectly delineated set. Such a notion conceptualizes search as an entirely transactional instruction with no interpretive element to it, like a library request slip instructing the retrieval of a specific volume from a specific location in the stacks. As we shall see, however, such procedural clarity describes only a small subsection of the operations that may be characterized as search, and, even then, there need to be interpretive critical protocols in place to decide how to disambiguate things. It should be no surprise to scholars of book history that there is more to the precision and accuracy of a library call slip than meets the eye. Metadata has to be created, fields standardized, ambiguities of bibliographical materiality and history resolved. The archives themselves have a history – they are mediated, contested processes rather than neutral, passive stores of material objects or information. Similar decisions have to be made, infrastructures built, data preprocessed and indexed before even the simplest of supposedly "unambiguous" computational operations of search-as-retrieval can happen.

In this section, I will interrogate some of the biases, assumptions, and uncertainties that lie behind search. Instead of thinking of search as primarily an instrumental interface that literary scholars need only to learn better to fully exploit its power, I shall argue that to use search at scale as more than a convenient retrieval aid, we need to get better at interpreting and critiquing the kinds of cultural ambiguities and statistical uncertainties embedded in it. This is not at all to say that learning to use the technology well is not important. However, becoming a power user who is good at using complex search patterns and finding particular texts or passages is only the first step in search. To use it not as a cursory tool in the research process but as an integral part of it, something we build critical insights on, report as part of our argument, and use to generate and think about trends and patterns, we have to think critically about the biases caused by the highly uneven distribution and survival rates of print in the early modern period, the cultural and statistical ambiguities embedded in the metadata, and the kinds of uncertainties generated by statistical language processing.[73]

## *Distribution*

A critical engagement with search is not possible without thinking critically about the underlying data – both as historically mediated and contested forms of textuality and as fundamentally complex computational objects. This is all the more true for a corpus like EEBO-TCP consisting of transcriptions of historical texts. These texts present some unusual technical challenges compared to modern corpora. Some are more obvious to scholars of the period than others. For example, early modern orthography is highly irregular, and syntax is evolving and in flux over this period. This poses particular challenges to modern language-processing algorithms, which are often trained on contemporary corpora where spelling is stable. In terms of computational representation, variant spellings are fundamentally different tokens – they need preprocessing to be resolved into versions of the same word. Moreover, when combined with early modern syntax, such language-parsing algorithms can produce some unexpected results. A modern part-of-speech tagger – a program that annotates the text with additional information, in this case parts-of-speech for each word – that failed to take early modern spelling into account, for example, struggled to annotate the phrase "wee doe" in The First Folio's rendition of *The Merry Wives of Windsor*: "We are simple men, wee doe not know what's brought to passe vnder the profession of Fortune-telling." The words "wee doe" were tagged as an adjective followed by a noun – in other words, "little deer." More persistent kinds of biases might occur as in the case where a simple search-and-tag program trained on a modern dictionary tagged all instances of "art" as a noun rather than mostly a verb in the EEBO-TCP corpus (rather than a form of "to be"). But better taggers trained on early modern language have rapidly improved the overall quality of linguistic parsing, and we are on the verge of a new generation of deep neural-network-based Natural Language Processing (NLP) models that

---

[73] In the following section I will use the term "bias" mostly in its statistical sense of a systematic deviation from expected value, especially in the form of a skew in a distribution.

promise to be even better. For example, the part-of-speech tagger used for the EarlyPrint project renders the modernization and parts-of-speech to "we do" correctly and displays it alongside a scan of a copy of the First Folio in the University of Pennsylvania library (Figure 1).[74]

Biases in tagging constitute relatively technical problems, and although humanists making large-scale statistical arguments using the corpus should be aware of them and how to account for these errors and biases, correcting them falls, by and large, into the technical domain of building better NLP models as part of our curation pipelines. There are other kinds of biases in the corpus, however, that require more sustained considerations of the historical specificity of the corpus and its social and political contexts. Figures 2 and 3 show the distribution of texts per year in EEBO-TCP in the form of black bars, along with texts in the online English Short Title Catalogue (ESTC) represented as gray bars, first across the entire period 1473–1700, and then zoomed in up to 1600. Since the EEBO-TCP aimed at encoding one edition of all texts printed in English or in England, Scotland, and Wales before 1700, it leaves out multiple (usually, but not always, second+), editions and certain categories of books such as catechisms, and, perhaps more problematically, treatises on music and scientific tracts as texts that presented particular encoding difficulties due to the heavy use of notations. Overall, this decision, while driven by economic exigencies in what was ultimately a massive and very expensive multidecade encoding project, has a collateral benefit of not introducing accidental biases into statistical studies of linguistic trends through repeated usages in reprints. It should be noted that such biases, while requiring an additional step or two, would have been easy to correct for, and even with the policy in place, certain categories of "reprints" – for example, late seventeenth-century editions of Chaucer – remain as sites of potential linguistic anomalies.

---

[74] A keen reader might notice that the rendering of the text is paired to a scan of a witness different from the one that was used to encode it (the EEBO-TCP encoding uses a copy of the First Folio at the Folger). The objective here, however, is to point the reader to the proprietary EEBO scans if they have access to ProQuest's database, but also to make available other witnesses of a text whenever possible.

*Page.* No, nor no where else but in your brain.

*Ford.* Help to search my house this one time: if I find not what I seek, show no colour for my extremity: Let them say of me, as jealous as *Ford*, that searched a hollow Walnut for his wife's Leman. Satisfy me once more, once more search with me.

*M. Ford.* What hoa (Mistress *Page*,) come you and the old woman down: my husband will come into the Chamber.

*Ford.* Old woman? what old woman's that?

*M. Ford.* Why it is my maid's Aunt of *Brainford*.

*Ford.* A witch, a Quean, an old cozening quean: Have I not forbid her my house. She comes of errands does she? We are simple men, we do not know what's brought to pass under the profession of Fortune-telling. She works by Charms, by Spells, by th' Figure, & such dawbry as this is, beyond our Element: we know nothing. Come down you Witch, you Hagge you, come down I say.

*Mist. Ford.* Nay, good sweet husband, good Gentlemen, let him strike the old woman.

*Mist. Page.* Come mother *Prat*, Come give me your hand.

*Ford.* Ile Prat-her: Out of my door, you Witch, you Ragge, you Baggage, you Poulcat, you Runnion, out, out: Ile conjure you, Ile fortune-tell you.

*Eua.* By yea, and no, I think the o' man is a witch indeed: I like not when a o' man has a great beard; I spy a great beard under his muffler.

*Ford.* Will you follow Gentlemen, I beseech you follow: see but the issue of my jealousy: If I cry out thus upon no trail, never trust me when I open again.

*Page.* Let's obey his humour a little further;
Come Gentlemen.

*Mist. Page.* Trust me he beat him most pitifully.

Figure 1 Combined interface for the First Folio. The left pane consists of an algorithmically modernized rendition of the EEBO-TCP encoding (also viewable in original spelling), and the right pane combines it with a zoomable scan.[75]

[75] Images in this Element are either screen-captures from "Early Modern Print: Text Mining Early Printed English," https://earlyprint.org/, or generated from the underlying databases and the TCP corpus.

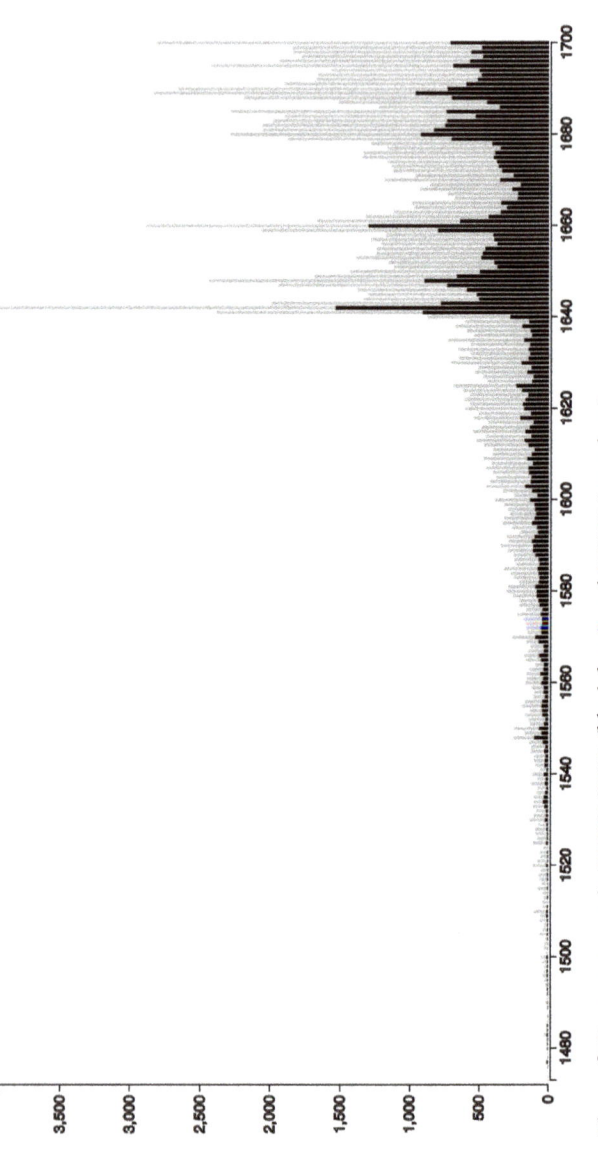

Figure 2 Texts per year in EEBO-TCP (black bars) and ESTC (gray bars).

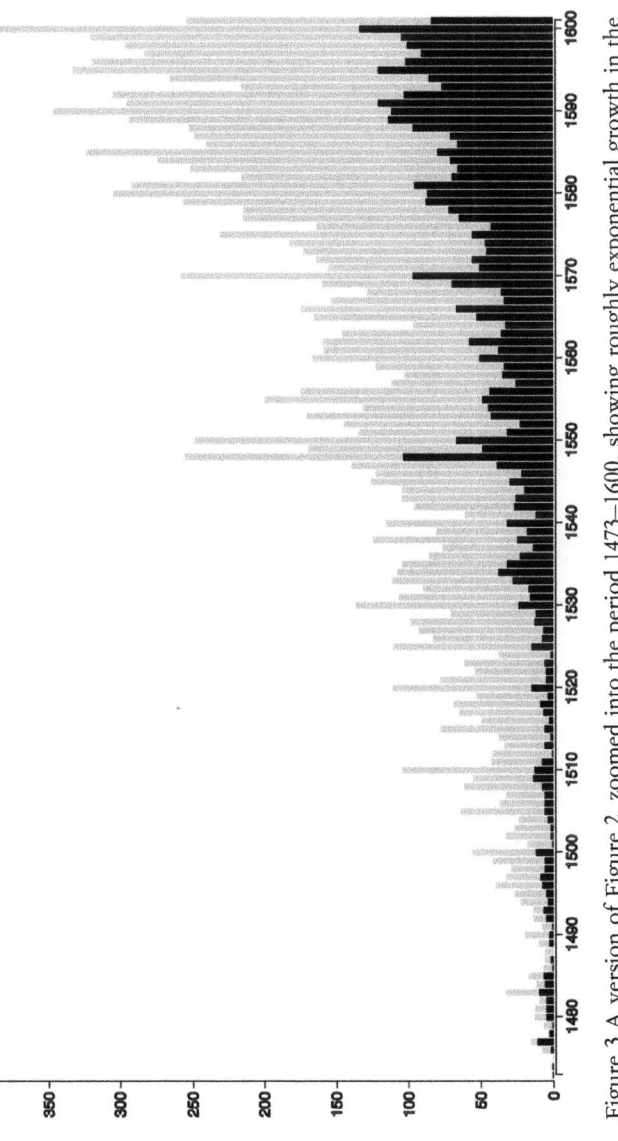

Figure 3 A version of Figure 2, zoomed into the period 1473–1600, showing roughly exponential growth in the number of books even in the earlier part of our period.

While the decision to focus on first editions and leave reprints out might be justified overall, the transcription of the earliest edition forecloses access to important information for scholars interested in the history and evolution of single texts. One such culturally significant text with an extensive history of emendations and additions through various reprints is John Stow's *Survey of London*. First printed in 1598, then again in 1603 in an enhanced edition by the author, the volume continued to attract wide interest well after Stow's death and saw significant additions and changes in the 1618 and 1633 editions, along with a long afterlife into the following centuries (Figure 4). To a historian of London, or to anyone interested in Stow's depiction not only of the geography and institutions of the city but also its changing social and political landscape, the differences between editions are vitally interesting, if not crucial. However, EEBO-TCP makes the decision to produce a transcription of only the 1633 edition as the most comprehensive. It is almost twice the length of Stow's original 1598 volume, but having just one edition in the corpus leaves no easy way to discern differences and additions. Even for statistical analysis, the choice of a single edition, especially of such a monumental volume, creates potential difficulties. It gives the impression that a sudden interest in London is concentrated in the fourth decade of the seventeenth century, an observation that might initially seem to corroborate other kinds of cultural activity around that period that might drive interest in the institutions of civic life in London. Such biases need a degree of what computer scientists often call "domain knowledge" – contextual knowledge about the importance and publishing history of Stow and awareness of other texts and modes of representing early modern London that would allow a historian, for example, to easily explain phenomena that might look like oddities if one had nothing but the "data" to go on. Any result extracted from the corpus at scale requires investigation into such possible biases and pitfalls, and thought about how we might interpret or correct them, taking into account both the historical circumstances of the data and the cultural contingencies and technical constraints under which the corpus was produced.

In corpus-based analysis, such domain knowledge is almost always necessary, no matter how statistically robust and based on hard empirical data the underlying search patterns seem. The bias, we must remember, is in

*Shakespeare and Scale* 55

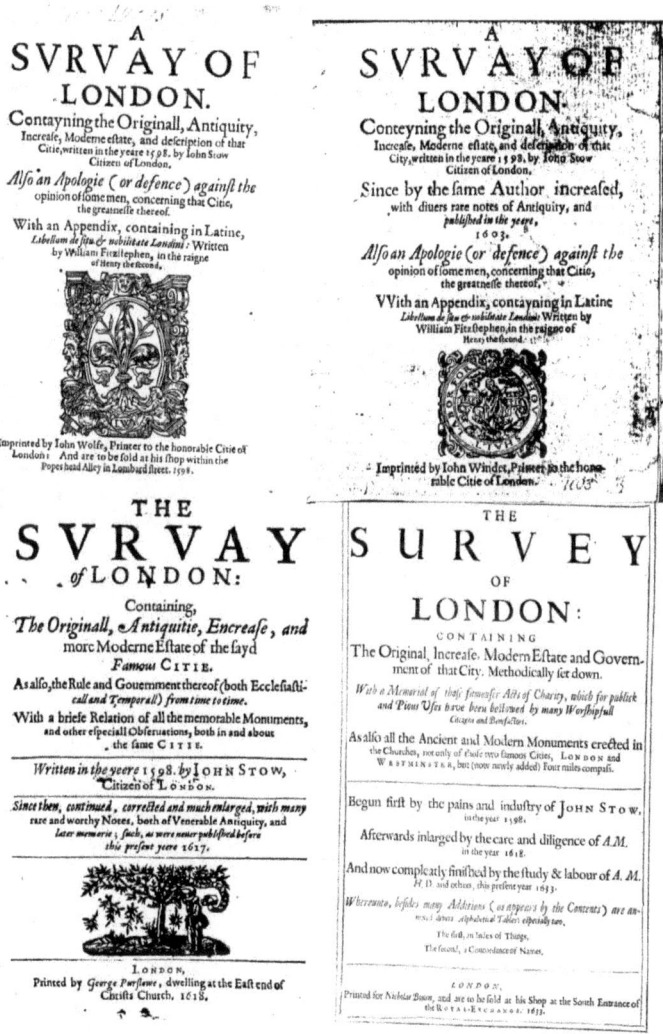

Figure 4 Title pages of the 1598 and 1603 editions of John Stow's *Survey of London*, along with the enhanced editions of 1618 and 1633.

the contingencies that shape the cultural field – the more than two centuries of early English print history on which we gaze when we trace patterns in EEBO-TCP. Print history is deeply contested, evolving, and adapting under myriad external and internal pressures. The patterns such processes leave behind are often observable by proxy in the material traces of textual culture. Even the simplest, most rudimentary aspects of book history, when quantified and visualized at scale, might bear witness to such patterns. However, we should never mistake the supposed "simplicity" of the data or the clarity of a pattern for a correspondingly simple causal pattern, or an explanation for why they occur. Consider, for example, the two panels of Figure 5. The top panel shows the number of texts in the EEBO-TCP corpus, essentially reproducing the darker bars from Figures 2–3; the bottom panel shows the number of words in the corpus per year. The overall trend makes the rate of growth of print starkly obvious – in fact, as Figure 3 demonstrated, zooming in on small portions of the timeline shows that the growth of print continues to hold roughly the same pattern of exponential growth throughout the period. Even at this very broad scale, and by such crude metrics as text and word counts, certain interesting patterns are visible. The most striking of these is the explosion of print around the period of the civil wars. But this is not necessarily an accurate depiction of the underlying growth or sudden cultural centrality of print. Rather, it is a manifestation of the contingencies of historical survival. What we are seeing is a distortion caused by the collection of civil war tracts by George Thomason, whose efforts ensured that these documents survived and were subsequently preserved in the Bodleian Library. Thomason's collecting of printed texts that might otherwise have been lost is a reminder that any observation about print we could make from this corpus – or from the ESTC, for that matter – is subject to the hazards of historical transmission and survival. It is quite likely that the number of books, pamphlets, broadsides, etcetera, being printed saw a significant increase in the years leading up to the civil wars and the interregnum, but that is not a claim we should hang solely on the evidence of this visualization. Consider what else this data might offer us in terms of insight. We might notice – by comparing the top and bottom panels of Figure 5 – that the rate of growth in the number of words over time is more even compared

*Shakespeare and Scale*

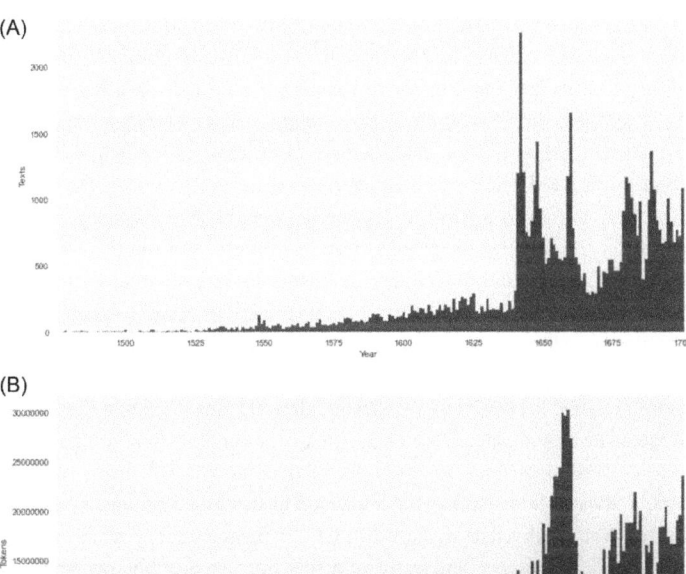

Figure 5 The number of volumes per year (panel A), and total number of words per year (panel B) in the TCP corpus.

to the number of texts. In other words, the average length of texts printed continues to increase more evenly, while there are certain windows where the number of texts printed spikes.[76]

[76] A quirk of bibliographical history and metadata creation might be kept in mind here. Notice that the first years of decades often tend to have small spikes. These are caused by the fact that when a text may not be dated to a precise year, it might be dated to a decade and, in the course of parsing metadata, such texts are gathered in the first year of the decade.

What happens, we might ask, to the length of texts during the spikes in print that also happen to correspond to periods of political upheaval? Figure 6 visualizes the number of tokens for each text on a log scale on the Y axis and the year on the X axis – that is, each incremental step along the Y axis represents a ten-fold increase or decrease in the length of texts. Over this is fitted a line representing the median length of texts. It turns out that there is indeed a drop in the median length of texts being printed, mostly corresponding to times of political unrest. We might now be on slightly firmer ground to claim, or at least to investigate, that what we are noticing in this pattern is the birth of something like a public sphere, where growing trust in print means people readily turn to it as a medium of debate, polemic, and persuasion – making their case through shorter political tracts, pamphlets, and broadsides. It would be relatively easy – using a spreadsheet of metadata downloaded from EarlyPrint, for example – to investigate what kind of texts contribute to these pronounced downward turns. And one should always do so before making broad claims based on data as difficult and uneven as the that of EEBO-TCP. It turns out that while political rhetoric did play more and more of a role in printed public debate in the seventeenth century, there are still some parts of the pattern that owe to the quirks of textual transmission. The drop in average length around 1570, while relatively pronounced and containing a fair few excoriations of Popish atrocities and such, owes substantially to the fact that several broadside (that is, single-page) ballads from the Huth Collection of the British Library were dated around then, thus pulling down the average length. The patterns we see, we must always remind ourselves, emerge under multiple complex and often contradictory historical and cultural forces. Data can draw our attention to possible sites of interest or anomaly, but should always be qualified with a nuanced evaluation of underlying biases, and a fundamental awareness of the unevenness of its distribution in the early modern corpus.

## *Metadata*

The anomalies and biases we have observed so far – from irregularities of spelling to the various accidents and aporias of book history that punctuate and constrain how we see the field of early modern

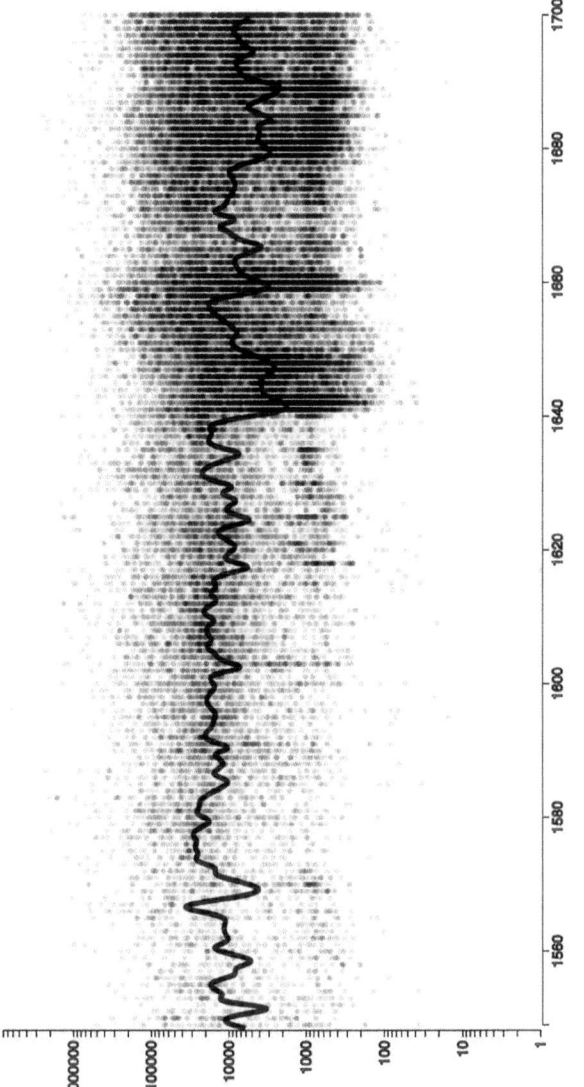

Figure 6 The number of words in EEBO-TCP texts from 1550 to 1700 plotted against the year of publication, with a median line fitted for the length of texts.

textual production – are the kinds of oddities that scholars are accustomed to in the course of research. These caveats might be couched in a veneer of objectivity created by well-tabulated results or data visualizations, but that is precisely why we need to problematize search and interrogate the idiosyncrasies of the underlying corpus. They are constant reminders of the irregularities of the field of print history. There are, however, still other kinds of uncertainty and bias to which we need to attend – ones that may seem to challenge precisely such scholarly knowledge of the cultural landscape. I will discuss under the rubric of "metadata" two broad categories of data associated with texts that bring with them, at the scale of the corpus, their own kinds of uncertainty. Metadata is often described as data about a text – data detailing the circumstances of the text's production and transmission, as well as bibliographical information about classifying or categorizing it. Often, metadata is treated as something outside the text – as supplementary information. Michael Gavin, while he deals with various kinds of metadata accompanying texts – "biographical, temporal, geographical, and lexical" – speaks of a broad division between "textual data [and] contextual metadata."[77] Such metadata, accumulated over long periods of time by many bibliographers, librarians, and curators, have their own history and present their own challenges for corpus curation. However, the linguistic preprocessing of corpora produces data that may be thought of as offset transformations of the corpus and is especially important for making a corpus as linguistically uneven (in terms of orthography and syntax) as EEBO-TCP tractable to computational processing. Such linguistic information may also be thought of as metadata – data about the text. Importantly, however, these data are often encoded into the text itself, meaning that we only access the "real" text through layers of such algorithmically generated metadata. For example, when we search for a modern spelling version of a certain word with the intention of finding all of its early modern orthographic variants, we are really searching for linguistic metadata generated by preprocessing the text instead of the text itself. The processing of both

[77] Gavin, *Literary Mathematics*, 8–10.

*Shakespeare and Scale* 61

bibliographical metadata and linguistic metadata introduces fundamental uncertainties into the corpus. But a lot of the time, scholars using such data either are not aware of such uncertainties because such uncertainties are not properly marked or clearly explained by projects, or they don't know how to interpret and report uncertainty in a robust way.

The first category of metadata – bibliographic metadata accompanying the corpus – is what is conventionally denoted by the term. In itself, as Gavin has argued, the collection of metadata is already motivated by a certain kind of perspective on print history – one that is fundamentally interconnected, forming a complex tapestry of interactions, coteries, and pathways of transmission:

> The catalogue provided a record system that made library holdings visible and therefore accessible. That visibility depended on translating archives to historical points of reference outside themselves: to authors, titles, imprints, catalog numbers, libraries, etc. Catalogues fold archives into history by layering them with historical metadata.[78]

The metadata that accompanies EEBO-TCP was originally derived from the short title catalogues of Pollard, Redgrave, Pantzer, and Wing, and supplemented by library-holdings data for the volumes that were included in the microfilm image archive that became the EEBO corpus. These records became part of the ESTC, which supplements them with helpful – if sometimes subjective and unevenly applied – subject categories which correspond to the Library of Congress subject headings. EEBO-TCP further adds to this information various details about its encoding procedure and supplies the metadata as XML-encoded headers. This process of transmission and the massive efforts required to collect the data, Pollard reminds us, inevitably introduced errors into it: "in so large a work based on such varied sources, probably every kind of error will be found represented, and those who use the book as anything more than a finding-list must be on

---

[78] Gavin, "How To Think About EEBO," 87.

their guard."[79] However, more than what may be narrowly defined as "error" – something that escaped attention, was omitted or mistranscribed, but if brought to attention, could reasonably be "corrected" – the historical processes of the creation and transmission of this vast body of metadata introduces uncertainty – that is, things that are matters of critical or cultural perspective, artifacts of geographic and historical location. The metadata accompanying EEBO-TCP represents layers of work by generations of scholars, bibliographers, and librarians working in very different geographic locations and cultural circumstances, from original readers and collectors to historical library archives, from bibliographers working to create functional card catalogs to those working with modern database protocols. Any use of the metadata must begin with a recognition not only of possible errors to be corrected but also of this baseline of inherited cultural subjectivity and uncertainty.

Over this base, is another, perhaps more structured and manageable (although, ironically, often more unsettling for scholarly users), layer of uncertainty. Many fields within EEBO-TCP's XML metadata are basically fragments of the title page of a volume broken into subsections. To extract basic organizing information such as date, place of publication, printer, publisher, bookseller, etcetera, requires quite a bit of complex and often semiautomated or even largely automated preprocessing. Such processes usually start by picking up obvious patterns, using a variety of computational processes – from simple regular expression-based string pattern matching to complex machine learning algorithms – to parse the data into regular, more tractable formats. Finally, as is inevitably necessary given the irregularities of early print history, a subset of the data that is either too irregular to parse or is flagged because it falls below some threshold of statistical certainty is identified for hand-curation. Most of these processes of scalable, computationally mediated data curation are too cumbersome and tedious to discuss in any detail here. But perhaps a few examples will illustrate the kinds of difficulties emerging from such processes and, in turn, allow us to think of how to negotiate the kinds of errors and uncertainties introduced by them.

---

[79] Quoted in Gavin, "How To Think About EEBO," 73.

Consider a few examples of entries made into the date field by bibliographers. For entries that might be difficult to parse because presented in Roman numerals, numeric dates are often noted alongside, although their providence and purpose are not always clear. The easiest of such interventions is when a numeric year is noted simply to clarify the original entry – for example, when "The yere of our lorde. M.CCCC.xxviij. the. vij. day of August the. xx yere of the reygne if our moost dradde souerayne and naturall kynge Henry the. viij. defender of the fayth" is helpfully resolved to "1528" in the metadata. It is possible to parse Roman numerals – even in their wildly variant early modern incarnations – computationally with a high degree of accuracy, but sometimes we are grateful for the helping hand a bibliographer provides in verifying the parsed date: "xxv.die mensis Septembris. Anno millesimo. CCCC. nonagesimo octauo [1498]." But in other cases such annotations by bibliographers do not exist, and, even if they do, their purpose and what authority we should attribute to them is not clear. Often a date is followed by a "?" denoting uncertainty, or a year range is noted but with little other information about how it was determined or how we should treat it. Is the uncertainty the result of a bibliographic feature of the microfilmed copy, such as the third edition of Stow's *Survey* (Figure 4), which mentions both 1617 and 1618? Does it represent a genuine scholarly uncertainty about the date of a text, or merely a cataloguer's hesitation to put a precise date on a text they might have been unsure about? These layers of uncertainty accrued over time are already folded into the metadata that accompanies EEBO-TCP. Other instances might look similar but require genuine individual inspection by someone familiar with the scholarly history of the text if our goal is to resolve a single accurate year of publication. When Elinor Channel's *A Message from God, by a Dumb Woman to his Highness the Lord Protector* declares the date of publication to be "Printed in the year 1653. Or as the vulgar think 1654," it probably lies beyond the reach of an algorithm to make a decision on what date we should note in the corpus.[80] A well-designed algorithm – one that accounts for

---

[80] "A message from God, by a dumb woman to his Highness the Lord Protector." Early English Books Online, https://name.umdl.umich.edu/A78569.0001.001 (accessed June 3, 2024). The author offers the following as explanation for the

some of the pitfalls of early modern print history – will know enough to flag such records for individual inspection, and a scholar could resolve the date relatively easily in this case, and others. However, any algorithmic intervention should accommodate constant iterative improvement. For example, an algorithm that was designed to resolve short date-spans into single dates for the purposes of tracing large-scale patterns should be able to flag texts that present significantly larger date-spans or unusual patterns. "The first publique lecture, read at Sr. Balthazar Gerbier his accademy, concerning military architecture, or fortifications" prints on the title page the obviously wrong date of 1469, an error that is corrected by a bibliographer with a terse "[i.e. 1649]": "Printed by Gartrude Dawson, and are to be sold by Hanna Allen at the Crown in Popes-head-alley, London : 1469. [i.e. 1649]." A well-designed algorithm should flag this as something to be inspected, or to trust the bibliographer's emendation over the printed date.

Dates, by and large, are among the more easily resolvable features of the TCP metadata. Other fields, especially metadata about printers, publishers, and booksellers, present harder challenges. The publication statement field in the EEBO-TCP metadata usually simply reproduces the original lines from the title page of a text with no indication of separating out names, let alone standardizing them or disambiguating them to a particular person. Properly curated, this data would open up immense possibilities for research into the history of early modern book culture. We might be able to trace networks of association between coteries or authors and particular constellations of actors in the marketplace of books. When combined with the full texts and other metadata fields, further avenues of exploration might come to light as well. In the next section, for instance, we will look at identifying specific habits of orthography as distinctive comparable vectors, replicating at scale some of the observations that have driven research into the distinctive habits of individual compositors. Being able to combine such

> oddity in dating: "And to make out unto you, that 1653 is not compleat from the Birth of Christ, untill the 25. of next December. Thus the 25. of March is the day of Christs Conception, die Birth is 9. Months after the Conception, so that if it was last 25. of March 1653. compleat from the Conception of Christ, it cannot be 1653. compleat from the Birth, until the 25. of December next."

analysis of language with metadata about printers at scale might allow us to study the material network of print at a level of granularity that has either been unachievable before or, as in the case of Shakespeare's texts, come about through centuries of sustained scholarship.

Despite this promise, such regularization requires the disambiguation of nearly 100,000 records and the development of statistical methods capable of processing the ambiguities of early modern texts. Names are parsed out from publication statements and standardized using a combination of spelling correction methods using orthographic patterns "learned" from the corpus, a set of procedures that translate between English and Latin versions of names, and clustering techniques that gather similar names together.[81] We can deduce, for example, that "John," "Iohannus," "Iohne," and their many variations denote versions of the same name. Similar techniques help us gather that the last name "Wolf" may exist in our metadata in several versions, including "Wolfe," "VVoolfe," etcetera. Combined with some consideration of the dates within which they operated, we can begin to cluster names into groups for relatively quick reviewing and the generation of unique Virtual International Authority File (VIAF) IDs.[82] Most processes of scalable curation, therefore, need a certain degree of computational and statistical intervention, as well as human attention at critical junctures. Such models need to pay close attention to the quirks of early modern print history to identify tractable patterns, but, most importantly, they are reiterative, designed to flag outliers and be repeatedly modified by curators.

## *Uncertainty*

In spite of our best efforts, any statistical model will have certain margins for errors and outliers. This is all the more true in the case of a corpus as vast and complex as the EEBO-TCP, consisting of nearly 1.7 billion tokens and representing more than two intensely contested and eventful centuries of

---

[81] For the use of machine learning to represent early modern spelling habits quantitatively and to learn "weights" for substitution for them, see the next section.

[82] "VIAF," https://viaf.org/ (accessed June 13, 2023).

early printed English. Whatever complex patterns we parse for, whatever nuanced models we build, we should expect to find at least a few examples in the corpus that defy their limits. Even the cursory examples in the last section should alert us to this fact that any experienced reader of early modern texts knows. Thus, to the already existing complexities of a corpus plagued with "every kind of error," as Pollard warns us, is added another layer: statistical error. Many scholars might lean toward treating a statistical error as more egregious than a human error or culturally accrued mistakes or aporias. But is this really the case? Are machine-generated errors categorically worse than human-generated ones? I would argue that this is the wrong question to ask. The rate of error in the corpus is not in itself problematic. But we need to be able, first of all, to flag and understand what probabilistically generated data represents and, secondly, to process and report the rate of errors and degrees of certainty in the corpus as we draw conclusions from it. We tend to think of errors as individual instances that have slipped through the cracks of the very intricate history of this corpus. However, we should distinguish at least two categories of what we might call "noise" in the corpus, to borrow a term from information processing. The first category, which I would call *bias*, consists of modes of error that arise from distortions in the data – either, as we have seen, from the peculiarities of its distribution or from the contingent historical circumstances of its production, transmission, or curation. I loosely borrow and adapt the term *bias* from its usage in statistical machine learning literature, where it denotes a model that is not quite ideally suited to fit the distribution of the data. While the distorted distribution of texts across the timeline of EEBO-TCP or the uneven distribution of words within the corpus gives rise to many potential situations where bias in this statistical sense would be introduced, I would suggest that the historical contexts of the accumulation and curation of these texts also introduce analogous forms of bias that can often be really hard to articulate. We have already discussed how rates of survival distort our view of the cultural field. Consider, moreover, how cultural perspectives, changing social norms, and tastes might all impact the survival and visibility of data. It is unlikely that various kinds of writing – women's writing, for example – survive and are collected, preserved, and cataloged at rates somehow unaffected by social attitudes. Taste, genre, prestige, and so forth obviously play significant roles in the popularity of editions, and thus the rates of survival.[83] More research into print runs, lost volumes, and the second-hand book market might ameliorate some of these blind spots, but it is key, when using a corpus like this to build arguments, to acknowledge such irregularities and perhaps find better ways of modeling the importance, social visibility, or reach we attribute to texts, concepts, or even words. Editorial theory has taught us to pay attention to the intricacies and instabilities introduced by sociohistorical processes. We should not forego those lessons when we are considering the metadata or the corpus itself at scale. If anything, those lessons take on new importance in accounting for unexpected sources of bias and blindnesses.

A second type of noise is introduced into the corpus specifically by statistical processing. We have seen the kinds of decisions that factor into the curation of metadata, but the text itself is also heavily mediated and preprocessed to make it accessible for reading and curation. Consider the reading text for Ben Jonson's poem first published at the start of the First Folio as rendered by the EarlyPrint Library (Figure 7). Panel A renders a screen shot of the transcribed text along with a zoomable scan of the page in panel B. Notice that hovering with the mouse on a word – "vvrit," in this case – brings up a floating window with some additional attributes of the word. The word has a unique identifier, allowing us to locate it exactly within the entire corpus. It also has a lemma – the form found in dictionary headwords – and a regularized or modern spelling along with, finally, a part-of-speech tag derived from the NUPOS tagset, which records "vvn," indicating that it is a past participle.[84] This gives us a glimpse of

---

[83] For a survey of recent work on lost books, see Alexandra Hill, *Lost Books and Printing in London, 1557–1640: An Analysis of the Stationers' Company Register*. BRILL, 2018. For a statistical approach to the estimation of lost print, see Leo Egghe and Goran Proot, "The Estimation of the Number of Lost Multi-Copy Documents: A New Type of Informetrics Theory," *Journal of Informetrics* 1, no. 4 (2007): 257–68.

[84] Annotations were generated using Philip R. Burns, "MorphAdorner," August 1, 2013, http://morphadorner.northwestern.edu/. For a discussion of morphadorner, see Anupam Basu, "MorphAdorner v2.0: From Access to Analysis,"

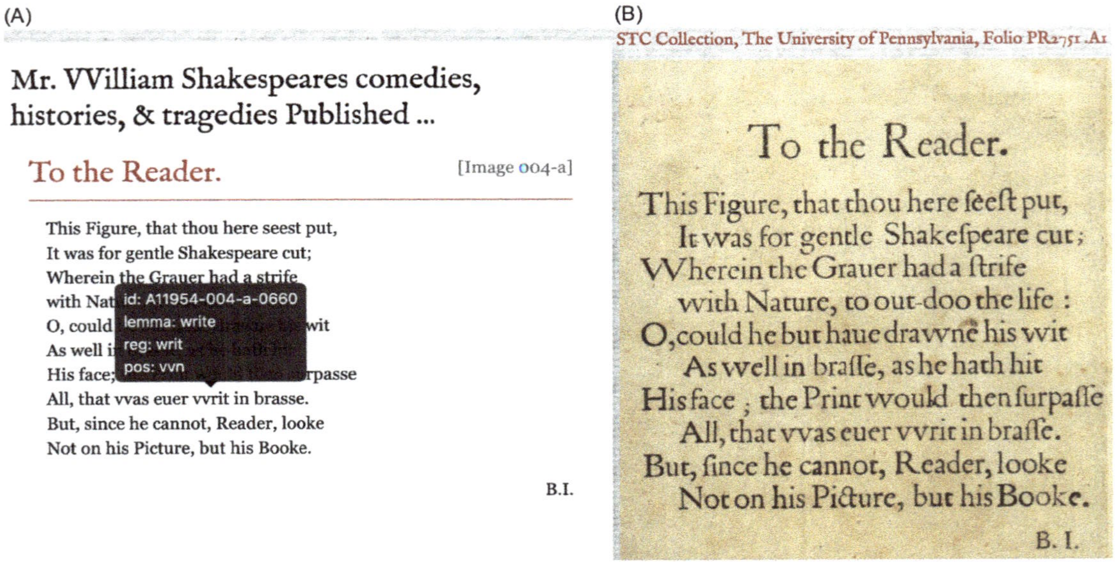

(A)

# Mr. VVilliam Shakespeares comedies, histories, & tragedies Published ...

## To the Reader.

[Image 004-a]

This Figure, that thou here seest put,
It was for gentle Shakespeare cut;
Wherein the Grauer had a strife
with Nat[ure, to our-doo the life:]
O, could he b[ut haue drawne his] wit
As well i[n brasse, as he hath hit]
His face; [the Print would then sur]passe
All, that vvas euer vvrit in brasse.
But, since he cannot, Reader, looke
Not on his Picture, but his Booke.

B. I.

id: A19954-004-a-0660
lemma: write
reg: writ
pos: vvn

(B)

STC Collection, The University of Pennsylvania, Folio PR2751.A1

## To the Reader.

This Figure, that thou here seest put,
It was for gentle Shakespeare cut;
VVherein the Grauer had a strife
with Nature, to out-doo the life :
O, could he but haue drawne his wit
As well in brasse, as he hath hit
His face; the Print would then surpasse
All, that vvas euer vvrit in brasse.
But, since he cannot, Reader, looke
Not on his Picture, but his Booke.

B. I.

Figure 7 Ben Jonson's encomium for Shakespeare in the 1623 First Folio, rendered in original spelling in the EarlyPrint Library.

the multiple states that underlie the original text that is encoded by the TCP. A toggled menu option allows the reader to switch to the modernized spelling version shown in Figure 8. It is important to note that this version of the text is extrapolated from the version in Figure 7 by a set of statistical processes. In other words, what we see on panel A of Figure 8 is a machine-generated version, consisting of the "reg" tags for words in the original text. The degree of this intervention is mostly hidden away from the user. In fact, the inattentive reader might not even notice which version they are looking at or, in turn, might assume that the regularized spelling version is the equivalent of any other modern edition of Shakespeare or perhaps an edited facsimile edition. There are some telling signs, however. We might note that the hyphenated "out-doo" in the fourth line was not correctly regularized. A look at the underlying XML might give us a better sense of how much of an intervention this curatorial step constitutes. Figure 9 show the XML encoding that comes from the TCP project. It is relatively sparse. It tries to capture basic formatting and original spelling, including, we might note, the use of the long s, something that is changed silently even in the original spelling rendition on EarlyPrint. Figure 10 is the equivalent XML generated by the EarlyPrint project using a program called Morphadorner for just the first four lines and the title. Each word in the corpus is parsed into multiple parallel tokens (the computational representation of a word), where each token has certain machine-generated attributes, including an identifier unique to this particular word within the corpus, a regularized form of the word, and a part of speech.

How is such a fundamentally computationally mediated corpus generated? More importantly, how should we think of and use such texts and report on the fundamental kinds of instability that are integral to their creation? As we have seen, the edition in Figure 8 does not quite do enough to indicate which parts of the text we are seeing are from the original encoding and which parts are statistically mediated. Even more

*Spenser Review* 44, no. 1 (2014), https://bit.ly/3Cih3cO. For a description of the NUPOS tagset, see Martin Mueller, "Nupos: A Part of Speech Tag Set for Written English from Chaucer to the Present," 2009, https://wordhoard.north western.edu/userman/nupos.pdf.

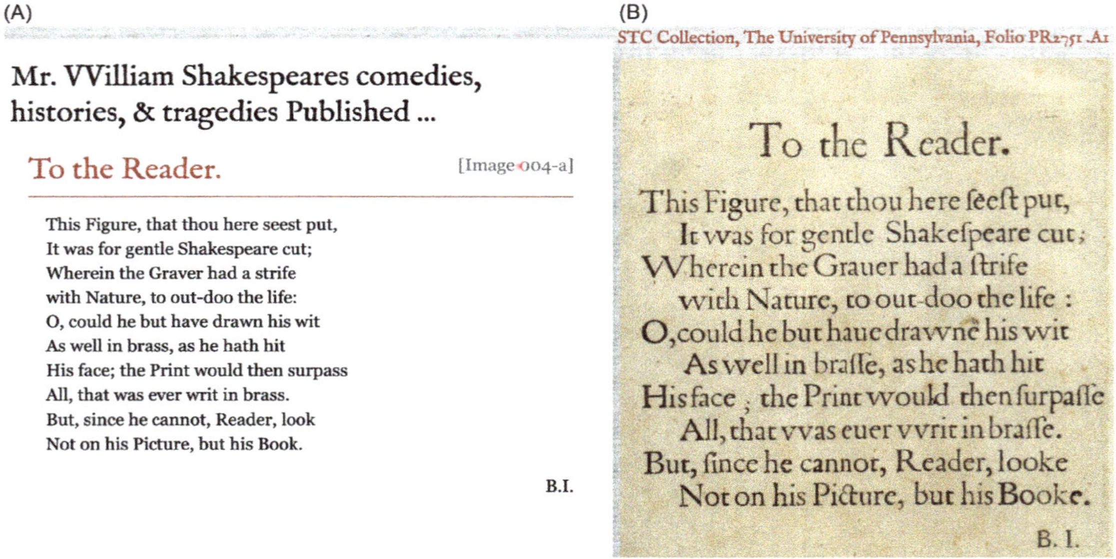

(A)

## Mr. VVilliam Shakespeares comedies, histories, & tragedies Published ...

[Image 004-a]

## To the Reader.

This Figure, that thou here seest put,
It was for gentle Shakespeare cut;
Wherein the Graver had a strife
with Nature, to out-doo the life:
O, could he but have drawn his wit
As well in brass, as he hath hit
His face; the Print would then surpass
All, that was ever writ in brass.
But, since he cannot, Reader, look
Not on his Picture, but his Book.

B.I.

(B)

STC Collection, The University of Pennsylvania, Folio PR2751 .A1

## To the Reader.

This Figure, that thou here seest put,
It vvas for gentle Shakespeare cut;
VVherein the Grauer had a strife
with Nature, to out-doo the life :
O, could he but haue drawne his wit
As well in brasse, as he hath hit
His face ; the Print would then surpasse
All, that vvas euer vvrit in brasse.
But, since he cannot, Reader, looke
Not on his Picture, but his Booke.

B. I.

Figure 8 Jonson's encomium, rendered in an algorithmically generated modern spelling version in the EarlyPrint Library.

```
<head>To the Reader.</head>
<l>This Figure, that thou here feeſt put,</l>
<l>It was for gentle Shakeſpeare cut;</l>
<l>Wherein the Grauer had a ſtrife</l>
<l>with Nature, to out-doo the life:</l>
<l>O, could he but haue drawne his wit</l>
<l>As well in braſſe, as he hath hit</l>
<l>His face; the Print would then ſurpaſſe</l>
<l>All, that vvas euer vvrit in braſſe.</l>
<l>But, ſince he cannot, Reader, looke</l>
<l>Not on his Picture, but his Booke.</l>
<closer>
    <signed>B.I.</signed>
```

Figure 9 TCP XML for the poem.

importantly, each token, when it is processed through a natural language-processing or machine-learning algorithm, is arrived at with a degree of certainty – with a probability value attached. If I might indulge for a moment to think of the machine as an interlocutor, a kind of digital research assistant who does the bulk of the work for us (not a far-fetched indulgence in the age of ChatGPT), we might imagine it saying something like the following: "I have compared the token 'vvrit' to its other uses in the corpus, and, having taken its immediate context, neighboring words, and syntactical structure into account, I can say with 91 percent confidence that its modern regularized form would be 'writ,' its lemma would be 'write,' etc." We might ask ourselves whether reporting this process and its confidence level would make the text better. From the perspective of a reader interested in a single text, it might not, since such a reader is concerned primarily with the generation of either an authoritative text to cite closely for scholarly work or an effective "good enough" reading edition. However, reporting probabilities, and especially clearly marking which aspects of the text are generated probabilistically, would make a crucial difference here, by marking out for scholars what the base layer of transcription is that might be cited without double checking with other

```xml
<div type="poem" xml:id="A11954-e10030">
 <pb facs="tcp:11596:1" xml:id="A11954-001-a"/>
 <pb facs="tcp:11596:1" xml:id="A11954-001-b"/>
 <pb facs="tcp:11596:2" rend="simple:additions" xml:id="A11954-002-a"/>
 <pb facs="tcp:11596:2" rend="simple:additions" xml:id="A11954-002-b"/>
 <pb facs="tcp:11596:3" rend="simple:additions" xml:id="A11954-003-a"/>
 <pb facs="tcp:11596:3" xml:id="A11954-003-b"/>
 <pb facs="tcp:11596:4" xml:id="A11954-004-a"/>
 <head xml:id="A11954-e10040">
  <w lemma="to" pos="prt" xml:id="A11954-004-a-0010">To</w>
  <w lemma="the" pos="d" xml:id="A11954-004-a-0020">the</w>
  <w lemma="reader" pos="n1" xml:id="A11954-004-a-0030">Reader</w>
  <pc unit="sentence" xml:id="A11954-004-a-0040">.</pc>
 </head>
 <l xml:id="A11954-e10050">
  <w lemma="this" pos="d" xml:id="A11954-004-a-0050">This</w>
  <w lemma="figure" pos="n1" xml:id="A11954-004-a-0060">Figure</w>
  <pc xml:id="A11954-004-a-0070">,</pc>
  <w lemma="that" pos="cs" xml:id="A11954-004-a-0080">that</w>
  <w lemma="thou" pos="pns" xml:id="A11954-004-a-0090">thou</w>
  <w lemma="here" pos="av" xml:id="A11954-004-a-0100">here</w>
  <w lemma="see" pos="vv2" xml:id="A11954-004-a-0110">seest</w>
  <w lemma="put" pos="vvn" xml:id="A11954-004-a-0120">put</w>
  <pc xml:id="A11954-004-a-0130">,</pc>
 </l>
 <l xml:id="A11954-e10060">
  <w lemma="it" pos="pn" xml:id="A11954-004-a-0140">It</w>
  <w lemma="be" pos="vvd" xml:id="A11954-004-a-0150">was</w>
  <w lemma="for" pos="acp" xml:id="A11954-004-a-0160">for</w>
  <w lemma="gentle" pos="j" xml:id="A11954-004-a-0170">gentle</w>
  <w lemma="Shakespeare" pos="nn1" xml:id="A11954-004-a-0180">Shakespeare</w>
  <w lemma="cut" pos="vvi" xml:id="A11954-004-a-0190">cut</w>
  <pc xml:id="A11954-004-a-0200">;</pc>
 </l>
 <l xml:id="A11954-e10070">
  <w lemma="wherein" pos="crq" xml:id="A11954-004-a-0210">Wherein</w>
  <w lemma="the" pos="d" xml:id="A11954-004-a-0220">the</w>
  <w lemma="Graver" pos="nn1" reg="Graver" xml:id="A11954-004-a-0230">Grauer</w>
  <w lemma="have" pos="vvd" xml:id="A11954-004-a-0240">had</w>
  <w lemma="a" pos="d" xml:id="A11954-004-a-0250">a</w>
  <w lemma="strife" pos="n1" xml:id="A11954-004-a-0260">strife</w>
 </l>
 <l xml:id="A11954-e10080">
  <w lemma="with" pos="acp" xml:id="A11954-004-a-0270">with</w>
  <w lemma="nature" pos="n1" xml:id="A11954-004-a-0280">Nature</w>
  <pc xml:id="A11954-004-a-0290">,</pc>
  <w lemma="to" pos="prt" xml:id="A11954-004-a-0300">to</w>
  <w lemma="out-doo" pos="j" xml:id="A11954-004-a-0310">out-doo</w>
```

Figure 10 Processed and statistically tagged XML for the first four lines of the poem.

sources. Access to information about textual transmission and mediation would be much more efficient.

But many other kinds of uses to which the text is put, including the bulk of what we might consider "search," is fundamentally dependent on the

Figure 11 Fields for corpus search on EarlyPrint.

transformed and, therefore, stochastic parallel states of the text. We need to remember that even the already complex XML rendition in Figure 10 is a highly simplified and static version of the ways in which this text is ultimately folded into the workings of the corpus. A look at the interface for corpus search gives us an indication of the basic affordances of indexing these parallel states (see Figure 11). We might subset our search by metadata fields such as author, title, or a range of years – ideally keeping in mind the potential ways in which those fields are already mediated. The other fields in the interface invite us to make full use of the statistically processed corpus. We may search the modern forms of a word without having to worry about anticipating all its early modern orthographic variants. We could qualify a word with a part of speech or reduce it to its lemma to catch all inflections. Going further, we could attend in new ways to the distribution not only of words in the corpus but of groups of words, syntactical structures, and repeated patterns. We can look for exact quotation or flexible allusion, the structures of particular rhetorical tropes and aphorisms, or the tendency of certain words to occur together to construct certain kinds of images. Daniel Shore has recently reminded us of the possibilities opened up by attending to syntax and pattern rather than particular words or sequences of words.[85] What the statistical processing of the corpus allows is the leveraging of patterns in complex ways: gradually moving away from the simple searching of words or static sequences

---

[85] Daniel Shore, *Cyberformalism: Histories of Linguistic Forms in the Digital Archive* (Baltimore, MD: Johns Hopkins University Press, 2018).

## Figure 12

| Before hit | word | After hit | Year | Author | Title |
|---|---|---|---|---|---|
| ... a decayed Library full of | **Pictures and Latin Titles of Books** | all which things when they ... | 1687-1700 | Knolles, Richard, 1550?-1 | The Turkish history from the o |
| ... Age to prefix their own | **Pictures to their Books** | but our present Writers much ... | 1700-1712 | Cervantes Saavedra, Migue | The history of the renown'd Do |
| ... that meditate is much like | **pictures in Books** | to Children they neglect their ... | | White, Thomas, Presbyteri | A method and instructions for |
| ... vnlearned men the same thynge | **Pictures are the bokes** | of vnlearned men that bokes ... | 1534 | Erasmus, Desiderius, d. 1 | A playne and godly exposytion |
| ... and the easier by this | **picture whiche I finde in euerie booke** | of the Sphere but that ... | 1556 | Record, Robert, 1510?-155 | The castle of knowledge |
| ... or nippers & teribilils whose | **pictures are in the Booke** | before named Also you shall ... | 1563 | Gale, Thomas, 1507-1587. | Certaine vvorkes of chirurgeri |
| ... of Sculpture aswell as of | **Picture excellent Artificers haue written great bokes** | in commendation Witnesse I take ... | 1570 | Euclid. | The elements of geometrie of t |
| ... be done to images & | **pictures the bookes** | and scriptures of lay men ... | 1571 | | The second tome of homilyes of |
| ... well by common deuises of | **pictures as by reprochfull Bookes** | and finally to assure him selfe ... | 1574 | | Articles conteining the reques |
| ... ceil you haue stolne my | **Pictures and ouerturned my Bookes** | If there be a priulledge ... | 1575? | Guevara, Antonio de, Bp., | The familiar epistles of Sir A |
| ... the honor of a grauen | **picture and the bookes** | which diligently he wrote were ... | 1577 | Eusebius, of Caesarea, Bi | The auncient ecclesiasticall h |
| ... forth anie enuious or spiteful | **pictures songs balades proses or bookes** | neither weare any markes or ... | 1579 | | The ordinance and edict, vppon |
| ... Greke signifieth the shape or | **picture of any thyng wherof his booke** | is ful And not as ... | 1579 | Spenser, Edmund, 1552?-15 | The shepheardes calender conte |
| ... on and thus shal the | **picture serue them in stede of bookes** | and helpe to procure inward ... | 1579 | Loarte, Gaspar de, 1498-1 | The exercise of a christian li |
| ... pictures in steede of printed | **Pictures ignorant mens bookes** | and therein beholde that passage ... | 1579 | Loarte, Gaspar de, 1498-1 | The exercise of a christian li |
| ... pictures in steede of printed | **Pictures ignorant mens books** | bookes and therein beholde that ... | 1579 | Loarte, Gaspar de, 1498-1 | The exercise of a christian li |
| ... meat the view of faire | **pictures the bookes** | of my study or the ... | 1579 | Gosson, Stephen, 1554-162 | The ephemerides of Phialo deui |
| ... an argument here of a | **picture neyther put in my booke** | nor by me deuised but ... | 1580 | Cranmer, Thomas, 1489-155 | An aunsvvere by the Reuerend F |
| ... Councel of Trent by the | **picture which was set before his booke** | as an argument of their ... | 1581 | Campion, Edmund, Saint, 1 | The great bragge and challenge |

Figure 12 Searching for "picture" followed by "book" within a five-word window.

for the mere retrieval of passages to a more open-ended exploration and engagement with the syntaxes and tropes of early modern language and also the development and evolution of ideas. For example, the last line of Jonson's Shakespeare poem (Figures 7 & 8) might stoke a curiosity about the association of "picture" and "book" (Figure 12), or perhaps a study on poverty might leverage the flexibility of the multiple states attributable to each token to search for "the poor" followed by a verb which produces a strikingly different set of results – talking about the poor as a category of people (e.g. "the poor lie in the ditches in London") – compared to searching for the word "poor" by itself (Figure 13), which will include uses such as "poor Tom."

*Shakespeare and Scale* 75

| Before hit | word | After hit | Year | Author | Title |
|---|---|---|---|---|---|
| ... by an other But for | the pore lay | man whiche can not haue ... | | Gilby, Anthony, ca. 1510- | An answer to the deuillish de |
| ... to restore in good helthe | the pour seek | folke languysshyng of their membris ... | 1483 | Jacobus, de Voragine, ca. | [Legenda aurea sanctorum, sive |
| ... hast formed to be lyche | The pore is | bore as is the ryche ... | 1483 | Gower, John, 1325?-1408. | tHis book is intituled confess |
| ... of Alexander & turned to | the poer releuys | of the lues vengyng hym ... | 1485 | | Here begynnys a schort [and] b |
| ... sleeth aswell the riche as | the pore soth | it is that ryghte many ... | 1491 | | [These ben the chapitres] of t |
| ... fede they theyre wyves Mar. | The pore had | ne breed and yet he ... | 1492 | | This is the dyalogus or co[m]m |
| ... of their wantonesse There shall | the pore accuse | the riche that wolde nat ... | 1493 | Mirk, John, fl. 1403? | The helpe and grace of almight |
| ... And yit god wyfle that | the pore take | rightnought of the goode that ... | 1493 | | Here endith a compendiouse tre |
| ... peas and of plente whanne | the pore hath | enogh or lightly may be ... | 1493 | | Here endith a compendiouse tre |
| ... is nat holpen therby & | the pore might | be holpen therby ful moche ... | 1493 | | Here endith a compendiouse tre |
| ... his state ne his richesse | The pore nedith | but lytel of alle this ... | 1493 | | Here endith a compendiouse tre |
| ... elbi necessaria The riche and | the pore been | ii thinges fulle necessarye eche ... | 1493 | | Here endith a compendiouse tre |
| ... in englissh The riche and | the pore mette | to themself the lorde is ... | 1493 | | Here endith a compendiouse tre |
| ... faders And he that yeueth | the pore shall | nat be pore sayth Salamon ... | 1493 | Mirk, John, fl. 1403? | The helpe and grace of almight |
| ... world yet rather gyue thenne | the pore be | vnseruyd Opyn thyn hert to ... | 1493 | Mirk, John, fl. 1403? | The helpe and grace of almight |
| ... syluer to gyue him Wherfore | the poore departed | fro theym without ony almesse ... | 1495 | | Vitas patrum |
| ... wyth good ryght tormented & | the peore comforted | in euerlastynge ioye ¶ Whan ... | 1495 | | Vitas patrum |
| ... compassion that he had toward | the poore solde | moche of theyr goodes & ... | 1495 | | Vitas patrum |
| ... ferre for the loue of | the pore Maye | ¶ O meruayllous prudence O ... | 1495 | | Vitas patrum |
| ... doo well ¶ And neuer | the poore departed | from her but if he ... | 1495 | | Vitas patrum |

Figure 13 Searching for the phrase "the poor" followed by a verb.

Many scholars have explored the emergence of new categories of thought and representation in early modern England in terms of a sort of linguistic displacement where an emerging concept is first articulated in terms of an inherited imaginative register before developing its own vocabulary and categories of representation.[86] To think of search as operating on multiple axes is to think of language at least partially in terms of such displacements, substitutions, and absences. As we learn to leverage the multiple parallel states that the corpus is processed into, we get better at thinking of search not only in terms of words or phrases to look for, but as patterns, associations, and correlations. Such progressive abstraction can

---

[86] This is a common form of argument in much early modern scholarship, but for examples of studies that specifically reflect on conceptual "blindnesses" and how they are often mediated by some form of linguistic displacement, see Subha Mukherji, ed., *Blind Spots of Knowledge in Shakespeare and His World: A Conversation* (Berlin: Medieval Institute Publications, 2019).

prove a powerful research tool where search is not only limited to retrieving particular texts but becomes an integral part of how we make arguments and report our results. But to be able to do so, we have to learn how to distinguish between the various kinds of noise in the corpus, how to interpret results drawn from such corpora, and, finally, how to report on such results and document such uncertainty.

I have already mentioned that corpus curators need to consider how different kinds of errors, biases, and uncertainty can be flagged in the corpus. At the very least, parts of the corpus – metadata, versions of texts, etcetera – that are the direct result of human intervention should be marked as such. Of course, "human intervention" can mean a wide range of things: from editor to encoder, from bibliographic researcher to catalog transcriber. Nevertheless, such biases are distinct from the statistically processed parts of the corpus and should be marked as such. On the other hand, we need to re-evaluate how we think of errors produced by statistical processes. Instead of approaching such errors in terms of individual mistakes that simply lower the quality of the data (they do), we need to learn to consider them in aggregate and make it a habit to report rates and possible sources of error. This becomes ever more crucial as we move from only close reading as a mode of scholarship to increasingly mixed and scalable models of reading. It is important to remember that our electronic texts are fundamentally mediated by the processes of transmission, curation, and statistical processing. Even if all we write on are single texts, the moment we search for a text or a word or encounter an electronically mediated database, we have irretrievably entered the realm of uncertainty, and we should be able to account for and report on it.

A simple statistical adage might be useful to remember: *trust the pattern, doubt the sample*. Statistical inference is designed to be accurate, even overwhelmingly so, in aggregate. It does not, therefore, imply that each individual sample can or should be trusted. We should, on the one hand, get more comfortable reporting trends, rates, and frequencies as information we can trust, albeit qualified by a certain error rate or confidence interval. On the other hand, we trust the evidence of statistically mediated metadata and individual texts far too naïvely and should always cross-check and verify individual elements drawn from a scalable corpus. The processes of statistical intervention become necessary due to the scale and complexity of the data. But, rather than thinking of this process as relinquishing a critical part of our scholarly agency to the obscurities of computation, we should rather think of it as reclaiming scholarly initiative. The critical scholarly currency is, after all, attention. By parsing the vast majority of texts relatively easily, such algorithmic intervention allows us to focus, often at massive scales and in terms of quite intricate patterns, on the aspects of early modern culture that really deserve our attention.

## 4 Praxis: Discovery

Under the broad categories of "digital" and "computational," I have tried to accommodate what might seem at first sight to be fundamentally different, even contradictory paradigms of thinking about the corpus. The digital text encompasses the hierarchical, procedural tasks that we most often associate with curation – the creation of digital facsimiles of texts that are as accurate as possible, along with an infrastructure for search and retrieval. However, as we have pushed at the speculative limits of search, the computational dimensions of such texts have come more into view – aspects that, while still strictly procedural, are fundamentally interpretive and radically transformative. Quantitative transformations might seem insurmountably reductive and incapable of accommodating nuance, yet they open up intertextual and comparative ways of seeing that capture subtle affinities and variations. The machinic logic that computation implements is precise, hierarchical, and, at the same time, capable of radical transformation and generative play. Moretti describes the gist of such transformation in terms of a tradeoff – simplification for the purpose of extracting broader patterns: "fewer elements, hence a sharper sense of their overall interconnection."[87] The first half of this formulation – reduction or simplification, which represents a facet of a text through a small set of empirically observable proxies – has received much attention. But we often remain skeptical about the other aspect of Moretti's claim – about how such simplification can extrapolate significant patterns. To a large extent, the sense of distrust about the second

[87] Moretti, *Graphs, Maps, Trees*, 1.

question arises out of our discomfort with the first. The reduction of texts to a small, somewhat arbitrary assortment of quantifiable features seems like a violence that is hard to look past for those trained to attend to the full richness of textual phenomena. Corpus curators, as well as scholars hoping to use the scale of the corpus for perspectives that allow the "sharper sense of their overall connection," need to take this discomfort seriously. To challenge the perceived incommensurabilities between distant and close, quantitative and qualitative, we need to accommodate the speculative, ludic, and generative modes of exploration as far as possible. However, we also need to demonstrate that the fear that scalable thinking can only function in a purely abstract, ahistorical register are unfounded. In fact, highly quantitative scalable approaches are not limited to verifying phenomena but can attend to the historicized, complex, and contested materialities of textual production and transmission.

## *Case Study: Speculative Search*

Much humanities research practice is inherently speculative. As we read widely and begin to get a sense of a cultural field, shaping structures and patterns emerge – first as shadows, hunches to explore, rabbit holes to fall into; then, gradually, as more concrete connections to trace, trends to verify, examples to collect. We move more often from hunch to persuasion than from hypothesis to proof. Serendipity plays a large part in this process – things that suddenly strike us in a new light, trails we had not picked up before, accidents of scholarly encounter. Humanistic reading and thinking, in this sense, is the tracing out of an ever more intricate network of connections rather than exhaustive, methodical, collection of data. In fact, much of the skepticism against empirical, quantitative approaches to criticism that we noted in the first section comes precisely from our reluctance to give up this intricate tapestry of persuasion for the dry rigor of proof. Our interactions with computers, however, even though they are an integral component of our research process, remain largely procedural: access, search, retrieval. Of course, easier access itself encourages exploration to some degree. Every scholar of early modern culture could probably recall things they came across and read while browsing EEBO that they would not have found or looked up had the only means of access been a traditional library. On the other hand, traditional libraries facilitate forms of speculative encounter that cannot be reduced to the dry procedurality of a search-and-retrieve query – for example, browsing the stacks or looking at adjacent items. At times, digital interfaces do try to mimic these modes in a digital medium, but those efforts are stunted, limited attempts, like page-turning effects on ebooks that coddle us with imitated familiarity. For example, many library catalogs allow users to browse items that are next to the search result on the shelves. As beneficial and productive as such encounter is, it is a happy fallout of digital media's ease of access. By and large, we don't actively use the affordances of computation to encourage or even enhance and extend such modes of serendipitous discovery. We are, however, alive, at least to some degree, to the radical possibilities of digital discovery and the modes of "browsing" it can open up. Most scholars are increasingly comfortable using Amazon recommendations as at least starting points for exploration. Consider to what degree we are getting comfortable with engines like Netflix allowing us to discover new things. Amazon and Netflix are leveraging the massive amounts of data available to them to simulate, in essence, the social coteries that traditionally have mediated taste and knowledge. Looking at Amazon recommendations – "people who like this book also liked . . . " – is the broad equivalent of having a discussion with a colleague who has overlapping interests about what to read next. But, because of its scale and the firm insistence on commercial ends, such recommendation systems always run the risk of establishing and reinforcing forms of normativity that we should be wary of.

What would a rethinking of humanistic serendipity in a truly computational register look like? What would it take to move away from – or to supplement – search as a technology of convenient retrieval and to reimagine it instead as a mode of open-ended discovery? We mostly think of search as a technology of nonsequential access where we more or less know what we want to retrieve. It can be something specific we are looking for, or we can search more expansively, as we saw in the previous section, to discover more general and complex patterns. In either case, search consists of relatively strongly coded prompts: "This is what I want to find; please bring me instances of this." We have seen a version of scholarly corpus search where a query for a word, phrase, or pattern is designed to retrieve *every* instance in the corpus that is a precise match. However, we sometimes approach search with very different expectations. Consider an undergraduate in a Shakespeare class researching references to magic in Elizabethan and Jacobean England. Being used to Google's paradigm, they might expect a list of texts that are "about" magic, sorted roughly by their "importance" or "relevance" to the topic. This requires a degree of modeling of cultural and critical assumptions about what constitutes importance, or about-ness, and most people would agree that there's more to importance than the simple repetition of a word.[88] Figure 14 displays the results of simply

0  1657 Naudé, Gabriel,  TCP # A89818
   *The history of magick by way of apology, for all the wise men who have unjustly been reputed magicians, from the Creation, to the present age. / Written in French, by G. Naudaeus late library-keeper to Cardinal Mazarin. Englished by J. Davies.*

1  1624 Carleton, George  TCP # A17971
   *Astrologomania: the madnesse of astrologers. Or An examination of Sir Christopher Heydons booke, intituled A defence of iudiciarie astrologie. Written neere vpon twenty yeares ago, by G.C. And by permission of the author set forth for the vse of such as might happily be misled by the Knights booke. Published by T.V.B. of D.*

2  1651 [no entry]  TCP # A97219
   *Magick & astrology vindicated from those false aspersions and calumnies, which the ignorance of some hath cast upon them. In which is contained true definitions of the said arts, and the justification of their practise, proved by the authority of Scripture, and the experience of ancient and modern authors. With observations from several remarkable conjunctions and apparitions: as those three suns that appeared before the Kings death, &c. / Impartially communicated for the publique good. By Hardick Warren, a well-wisher to the most secret occult arts and learning.*

3  1680 [no entry]  TCP # A25331
   *The Anatomy of transubstantiation*

4  1680 Son of the Church  TCP # A57614
   *Rome's overthrow in a fatal blow at her greatest idol, which leaves all inexusable who resolve still to be blind after such plain conviction a discourse very seasonable for these times wherein popery doth daily threaten in the nation / by a son of the Church.*

5  1652 Gaule, John, (1604?-1687.)  TCP # A42502
   *Pus-mantia the mag-astro-mancer, or, The magicall-astrologicall-diviner posed, and puzzled by John Gaule ...*

6  Greene, Robert  TCP # A02128
   *The honorable historie of Frier Bacon, and Frier Bongay. As it was lately plaid by the Prince Palatine his Seruants. Made by Robert Greene, Master of Arts.*

7  1665 Agrippa von Nettesheim, Heinrich Cornelius  TCP # A26564
   *Henry Cornelius Agrippa his fourth book of occult philosophy of geomancie, magical elements of Peter de Aban : astronomical geomancie ; the nature of spirits ; Arbatel of magick ; the species or several kindes of magick / translated into English by Robert Turner.*

8  1655 Agrippa von Nettesheim, Heinrich Cornelius,  TCP # A26563
   *Henry Cornelius Agrippa's fourth book of occult philosophy and geomancy magical elements of Peter de Abano : astronomical geomancy : the nature of spirits : and Arbatel of magick / translated into English by Robert Turner ...*

9  1594 Greene, Robert,  TCP # A02127
   *The honorable historie of frier Bacon, and frier Bongay As it was plaid by her Maiesties seruants. Made by Robert Greene Master of Arts.*

Figure 14 Ranked results for "magic."

[88] One might note that the asymptotic distribution of words in natural language corpora as defined by Zipf's law renders even the consideration of simple word counts somewhat complex in texts of different lengths and with different vocabulary ranges. See, for example, Sander Lestrade, "Unzipping Zipf's Law," *PLOS ONE* 12, no. 8 (August 9, 2017): e0181987, https://doi.org/10.1371/journal.pone.0181987.

searching for the word "magic" in the EEBO-TCP corpus, but instead of retrieving every instance of the specific word, the list of results displays a ranked list of documents that are likely to be about magic.

There are several key conceptual assumptions behind the computational transformations being performed in the search for "magic."[89] The BM25 weighting algorithm used to rank these results is broadly comparable to the tf-idf formula we explored in the first section. It associates a certain degree of "importance" to each word in a text by computing a "weight" for it. It takes into account the average length of documents in the corpus and the distribution of the term being queried – in other words, how localized to certain documents the term is – along with its frequency. This perspective, we notice, is fundamentally intertextual. A term's "importance" emerges only when we can compare it to a vast field of texts and judge its centrality in a single document in terms of its comparative rarity across the corpus. The transformation of the text in question here is relatively simple in itself. The challenge comes from the scale of implementing it as a near-instantaneous query over a corpus of 65,000 texts and 1.7 billion words. The key point is that, conceptually speaking, such a comparative and intertextual perspective poses a fundamentally different kind of question and requires a much more interpretive, subjective notion of importance or relevance. (After all, there are many other weighting schemes available that can articulate other conceptions of importance.) As such, ascribing "importance" to a term requires a different information architecture than the kinds of search we have encountered before.[90]

To collapse such significant conceptual and structural differences into a single rubric of "search" – a technological black box whose qualitative

---

[89] The search engine uses Apache Lucene to index the corpus and the results are weighted using the BM25 weighting scheme. See Christopher D. Manning, Prabhakar Raghavan, and Hinrich Schütze, *Introduction to Information Retrieval* (Cambridge: Cambridge University Press, 2008), 209.

[90] For an overview and comparison of various ranking and weighting methodologies, see Ronan Cummins and Colm O' Riordan, "Evolving Local and Global Weighting Schemes in Information Retrieval," *Information Retrieval* 9 (2006): 311–30, https://doi.org/10.1007/s10791-006-1682-6.

assumptions are opaque to us – is to ignore the critical and interpretive dimensions embedded in the quantitative articulation of such techniques and the degree to which computational texts can accommodate them. One of the key affordances of computation might be thought of as a kind of tedious, insistent "attention" that a human reader, no matter how alert, is simply incapable of sustaining at the scale of the corpus. Such "attention" can be leveraged to trace out trends and subtle patterns of correlation, slight inconsistencies and anomalies, which, in the aggregate, can allow us to move beyond the limitations of what I have called the "strongly coded prompt." In other words, instead of telling the algorithm exactly what words, phrases, or patterns we want to look for, we can provide it with an example of the *kind of thing* we are interested in and allow the search engine to interpret this query rather more broadly and interpretively. We are, of course, more often interested in concepts or thematic and formal structures rather than particular words. In fact, when we search for individual words, we often hope that they would pull up, along with their own instances, examples of their associations. Consider a scholar, for example, who is researching the early modern subgenre of pamphlets called the "rogue pamphlets" – works that purportedly warn honest citizens of the threat posed by the growing number of lawless vagrants and criminals. These texts register this threat in terms of the spatial as well as semiotic and economic mobility of these vagrants, outlining a portrait of a parallel, shadow society with its own norms, codes, and language. But, in spite of their tone of moral condemnation, these pamphlets have a comic element – they end up celebrating the wiles and merry adventures of these shifty rascals. Part sociology, part moral tract, part jestbook – rogue pamphlets, somewhat like their subjects, are a slippery genre to pin down.[91] So, too, is

[91] On the slipperiness of the genre and the problems of defining it, see Linda Woodbridge, "Jest Books, the Literature of Roguery and the Vagrant Poor in Early Modern England," *English Literary Renaissance* 33, no. 2 (2003): 201–10; Craig Dionne and Steve Mentz, eds., *Rogues and Early Modern English Culture* (Ann Arbor: University of Michigan Press, 2004); and Ari Friedlander, *Rogue Sexuality in Early Modern English Literature: Desire, Status, Biopolitics* (Oxford: Oxford University Press, 2022).

their language, which is pervasive in much early modern literature, in spite of the fact that rogue-books develop a very specific vocabulary and often attach word lists and glossaries. How might we go about exploring the spread and evolution of the language of roguery – the extent to which it pervades such vastly diverse early modern texts, especially in the comic register? One might begin by searching the corpus for the word "rogue" and maybe a few associated terms drawn from one's reading. But what one is actually doing in these searches is hoping that this limited entry point into the genre will draw out a richer tapestry of terms, the shifting conceptual landscape that we want to reach but can only gesture at with the very limited prosthetic that conventional search affords us.

Let me sketch out briefly two somewhat more speculative technical interventions that might fit the spirit of our query better. We are interested in expanding our initial limited set of keywords to a broader constellation of terms more representative of the imaginary register of the genre. But, beyond that, we might be interested in identifying passages where the language of roguery emerges, in its various guises and associations, as a thematic element. We might use a technique that has gained a lot of attention in recent years: word vectors, or semantic vectors.[92] These terms refer to an algorithm that takes advantage of the fact that semantically related words tend to occur with the same neighbors. While the technical implementation of word vectors is rather involved, its basic intuition is a simple one. Words with particular meanings tend to be associated with other words and often co-occur in the same contexts. A somewhat oversimplified example: if someone were to mention the word "python," we might, without other context, be unclear

---

[92] See Tomas Mikolov, Ilya Sutskever, Kai Chen, et al., "Efficient Estimation of Word Representations in Vector Space," *arXiv:1301.3781 [Cs]* (January 16, 2013), http://arxiv.org/abs/1301.3781; and Maria Antoniak and David Mimno, "Evaluating the Stability of Embedding-Based Word Similarities," *Transactions of the Association for Computational Linguistics* 6 (2018): 107–19, https://doi.org/10.1162/tacl_a_00008. For a discussion of word vectors in a literary context, see Michael Gavin, "Vector Semantics, William Empson, and the Study of Ambiguity," *Critical Inquiry* 44, no. 4 (2018): 641–73, https://doi.org/10.1086/698174.

whether the person was speaking of a snake or a programming language. But just a few additional words would disambiguate this to quite a high degree. If we hear "coil" or "habitat" occurring in the sentence, the likelihood that the person is talking of a reptile becomes quite high, while any mention of "data" or "variable" would equally swing the probability the other way. Conversely to this logic, words that have broadly similar meanings will tend to share similar associations. We would expect a preponderance of "data" and "variable" if we were talking of Java or C++ instead of Python because they are all programming languages and are discussed in broadly similar contexts. Word vectors make this insight tractable through a particular algebra that allows us to treat conceptual spaces in terms analogous to mathematical operations.[93]

So, given a set of keywords, we can extract their closest "neighbors" in this "vector space" and potentially curate the resulting list of terms to best reflect our critical goals. If we start with a set of common keywords often associated with the genre – "rogue," "cozener," "peddler" – we end up with the following list of terms (somewhat curated to eliminate very low-frequency words and spelling variations):

> arrant bawd beguile blockhead brothel cheat cog coney coni-catcher courtesan coxcomb cozenage cutpurse deceive disguise gull gypsy harlot juggler knave liberty mountebank pander pedlar pettifogger pickpocket pimp punk quack quean rakehell rascal scoundrel sin slave strumpet varlet villain wheedle whore witch

While by no means exhaustive, this preliminary query extracts an impressive core vocabulary, perhaps including a few words that might have otherwise escaped our attention. When we look for passages with a high concentration of this language instead of searching for individual words, a slightly different set of texts emerges that we might not have encountered using single keywords or phrases. Moreover, this approach focuses on

---

[93] The archetypal example often used to illustrate this point is "king" – "man" + "woman" = "queen" in Mikolov et al., "Efficient Estimation," 2.

shorter passages within texts rather than entire texts about a topic. These results include some expected texts: rogue pamphlets by Robert Greene and Thomas Dekker; works where urban spaces feature strongly, such as those by Thomas Nashe, John Taylor, and Samuel Rowlands; even some dictionaries or texts that have dictionary-like sections in them, such as John Wilkins' *An Essay Towards a Real Character, and a Philosophical Language* (1668). Translations of Rabelais also expectedly throw up some interesting passages.

Perhaps more interesting, because less expected, were a couple of passages from Shakespeare registering relatively high scores (i.e. that come up as high-ranking matches). The first was the section from *King Lear* where Kent fights Oswald while hurling abuse at him before being put in the stocks (II.ii14–40). The second was the following passage from *The Comedy of Errors*:

> Upon my life, by some device or other
> The villain is o'er-raught of all my money.
> They say this town is full of cozenage,
> As, nimble jugglers that deceive the eye,
> Dark-working sorcerers that change the mind,
> Soul-killing witches that deform the body,
> Disguised cheaters, prating mountebanks,
> And many such-like liberties of sin:
> If it prove so, I will be gone the sooner.
> I'll to the Centaur, to go seek this slave:
> I greatly fear my money is not safe. (I.ii.98–108)

Antipholus of Syracuse, alone and distraught, rages at the dangers lurking in Ephesus and, in doing so, briefly falls into the language so often used to describe the villanies of rogues in, for example, the pamphlets of Robert Greene, which describe early modern London as a bustling metropolis infested with various kinds of criminals and villains, which were also written around the same time as Shakespeare's play. *The Comedy of Errors* would be unlikely to be considered by someone focusing mainly on rogue-books, but the tropes created within the genre trickle down and tint Shakespeare's language in a variety of ways – ways that an increasingly broader conception of search can allow us to model and explore.

We could build even more accommodative, flexible, and abstract models to facilitate such serendipitous encounter and discovery. Imagine a sort of "Amazon for Early Modern Texts." It would take as input an exemplary text and generate a list of texts that are similar to it, given some interpretive criteria. Figure 15 shows the results of such a search using Robert Greene's *The Second Part of Cony-Catching* (1592) as our exemplary text. This set of results is extracted through much technical mediation involving modeling, text-processing, the building of precomputed distance matrices and databases, and so forth. And it uses, of course, the empirically tractable facets of these texts, including vocabulary, distribution, and structure. However, it is key to remember that this is by no means an "objective" ranking – it is a deeply interpretive one, which depends completely on the critical assumptions about language and culture we have embedded into the model. On EarlyPrint, we call this search interface the *Discovery Engine* to emphasize the serendipitous, unexpected, and, to a certain degree, arbitrary encounters it encourages. For example, Figure 16 runs the same search based on a distribution of topics instead of a distribution of weighted keywords. That is, instead of emphasizing two texts sharing significant keywords – something which stresses linguistic coteries and genre-specific jargon – it emphasizes the overall distribution of "topics," or conceptually related clusters of terms that tend to co-occur throughout the corpus.[94] These models make somewhat similar assumptions, so their results have a significant degree of overlap. There are interesting differences, though, that might spur further investigation. Since the keyword-based ranking in Figure 14 privileges distinctive vocabulary, Dekker, who picks up Greene's technical vocabulary and describes the various canting terms and modes of

---

[94] The scores in Figure 14 are generated using TF-IDF weighted vectors, while those in Figure 2 are generated from a set of topic model vectors. On topic modeling, or Latent-Dirichlet Allocation (LDA), see David M. Blei, "Introduction to Probabilistic Topic Models," *Communications of the ACM* (2011), and Lisa M. Rhody, "Topic Modeling and Figurative Language," *Journal of Digital Humanities* 2, no. 1 (2012).

| | | |
|---|---|---|
| 1591 | Greene, Robert, 1558?-1592.\|Greene, | The second part of conny-catching Contayning the discovery of certaine wondrous coosenages, either |
| 1592 | Greene, Robert, 1558?-1592. | A disputation, betweene a hee conny-catcher, and a shee conny-catcher whether a theefe or a whoore, is most |
| 1592 | Greene, Robert, 1558?-1592.\|Greene, | The third and last part of conny-catching With the new deuised knauish arte of foole-taking. The like coosnages |
| 1615 | Greene, Robert, 1558?-1592. | Theeues falling out, true-men come by their goods: or, The belman wanted a clapper A peale of new villanies rung |
| 1592 | Greene, Robert, 1558?-1592. | The defence of conny catching. Or A confutation of those two iniurious pamphlets published by R.G. against the |
| 1592 | Greene, Robert, 1558?-1592. | A notable discouery of coosenage Now daily practised by sundry lewd persons, called connie-catchers, and |
| 1608 | Dekker, Thomas, ca. 1572-1632. | The belman of London Bringing to light the most notorious villanies that are now practised in the kingdome. |
| 1607 | Dekker, Thomas, 1572- | Iests to make you merie with the coniuring vp of Cock VVatt, (the walking spirit of Newgate) to tell tales. Vnto |
| 1596 | Hutton, Luke, d. 1596. | The blacke dogge of Newgate both pithie and profitable for all readers. |
| 1638 | Hutton, Luke, d. 1596.\|Rowlands, | The discovery of a London monster, called, the blacke dogg of New-gate profitable for all readers to take heed |
| 1592 | Greene, Robert, 1558?-1592. | The blacke bookes messenger Laying open the life and death of Ned Browne one of the most notable cutpurses, |
| 1602 | Rowlands, Samuel, 1570?-1630? | Greenes ghost haunting conie-catchers wherein is set downe, the arte of humouring. The arte of carrying stones. |
| 1609 | Pasquil.\|Fennor, William, attributed | Pasquils iestes mixed with Mother Bunches merriments. Whereunto is added a bakers doozen of guiles. Very |
| 1679 | Burton, Robert, 1577-1640. | Versatile ingenium, The Wittie companion, or Jests of all sorts. From citie and countrie, court and universitie. : |
| 1661 | W. N. | Merry drollery, or A Collection of [brace] jovial poems, merry songs, witty drolleries intermix'd with pleasant |
| 1675 | Head, Richard, 1637?-1686? | Nuge venales, or, Complaisant companion being new jests, domestick and forreign, bulls, rhodomontados, |
| 1668 | Head, Richard, 1637?-1686? | The English rogue described, in the life of Meriton Latroon, a witty extravagant Being a compleat discovery of the |
| 1667 | Poor Robin.\|Winstanley, William, 1628? | Poor Robin's jests: or, The compleat jester Being a collection of several jests not heretofore published. Now newly |
| 1592 | Harman, Thomas, fl. 1567.\|Greene, | The groundworke of conny-catching, the manner of their pedlers-French, and the meanes to vnderstand the |
| 1674 | | The Complaisant companion, or, New Jests, witty reparties, bulls, rhodomontado's, and pleasant novels |
| 1687 | Crouch, Humphrey, fl. 1635- | England's jests refin'd and improv'd being a choice collection of the merriest jests, smartest repartee's, wittiest |
| 1661 | Phillips, John, 1631-1706.\|E. M.\|J. M. | Wit and drollery joviall poems / corrected and much amended, with new additions, by Sir J.M. ... Sir W.D. ... and |
| 1693 | Crouch, Humphrey, fl. 1635-1671. | England's jests refin'd and improv'd being a choice collection of the merriest jests, smartest repartees, wittiest |
| 1630 | Armstrong, Archie, d. 1672, attributed | A banquet of ieasts. Or Change of cheare Being a collection of moderne jests. Witty ieeres. Pleasant taunts. Merry |

Figure 15 Recommended texts most similar to Greene's *The Second Part of Cony-Catching*, based on weighted keyword distributions.

|  |  |  |
|---|---|---|
| 1591 | Greene, Robert, 1558?-1592. | The second part of conny-catching Contayning the discouery of certaine wondrous coosenages, either |
| 1592 | Greene, Robert, 1558?-1592. | A notable discouery of coosenage Now daily practised by sundry lewd persons, called connie-catchers, and |
| 1592 | Greene, Robert, 1558?-1592. | The blacke bookes messenger Laying open the life and death of Ned Browne one of the most notable cutpurses, |
| 1592 | Greene, Robert, 1558?-1592. | The defence of conny catching. Or A confutation of those two iniurious pamphlets published by R.G. against the |
| 1592 | Greene, Robert, 1558?-1592. | A quip for an vpstart courtier: or, A quaint dispute betweene veluet breeches and cloth-breeches Wherein is |
| 1592 | Greene, Robert, 1558?-1592. | A quip for an vpstart courtier: or, A quaint dispute betweene veluet breeches and clothbreeches Wherein is |
| 1676 | Wade, John, fl. 1660-1680. | The crafty maid of the west: or, The lusty brave miller of the western parts finely trapan'd. A merry new song to |
| 1605 | Tourneur, Cyril, 1575?-1626. | Laugh and lie downe: or, The worldes folly |
| 1602 | Rowlands, Samuel, 1570?-1630? | Greenes ghost haunting conie-catchers wherein is set downe, the arte of humouring. The arte of carrying stones. |
| 1575 | Awdelay, John, fl. 1559-1577. | The fraternitye of vacabondes As wel of rufflyng vacabondes, as of beggerly, of women as of men, of gyrles, as of |
| 1668 | | A pleasant new ballad of the Miller of Mansfield in Sherwood and how he was lodged at a millers house, and their |
| 1681 | Wade, John, fl. 1660-1680. | The subtile damosel: or, Good counsel for maids. Wherein she shews to every maiden fair, to take heed of false |
| 1660 | Deloney, Thomas, 1543?-1600. | The honour of the gentle craft a discourse of mirth and wit to the renown of those two princes Crispine and |
| 1676 | | The Crafty maid of the west, or, The Lusty brave miller of the western parts finely trapan'd a merry new song to |
| 1609 | Pasquil.|Fennor, William, attributed | Pasquils iestes mixed with Mother Bunches merriments. Whereunto is added a bakers doozen of guiles. Very |
| 1595 | Oat-meale, Oliver. | A quest of enquirie, by women to know, whether the tripe-wife were trimmed by Doll yea or no Gathered by |
| 1685 | | The London lasses folly, or, The maiden beguil'd to the tune of The iourney-man shooe-maker. |
| 1640 | | A pleasant new ballad of the Miller of Mansfield, in Sherwood and of King Henry the second, and how he was |
| 1592 | Harman, Thomas, fl. 1567.|Greene, | The groundworke of conny-catching, the manner of their pedlers-French, and the meanes to vnderstand the |
| 1588 | | [A Ballad of King Henry II and the miller of Mansfield] |
| 1613 | Tarlton, Richard, d. 1588, attributed | Tarltons iests Drawne into these three parts. 1 His court-wittie iests 2 His sound cittie iests. 3 His country prettie |
| 1632 | | The Countrey mans chat wherein you shall finde how each man doth talke to please his owne minde : to the tune |
| 1607 | Dekker, Thomas, ca. 1572- | Iests to make you merie with the coniuring vp of Cock VVatt, (the walking spirit of Newgate) to tell tales. Vnto |

Figure 16 Recommended texts most similar to Greene's *The Second Part of Cony-Catching*, based on topic distributions extracted with LDA.

crimes such cony-catchers or conmen indulge in, ranks very highly in the list – right after Greene himself. But, as we modify the perspective to the distribution of topics in Figure 15, other texts that might not share vocabulary as closely but perhaps share more of Greene's storytelling flare or humorous style climb up the list. And other rankings – other ways of organizing the texts using slightly different interpretations of what makes a text "important" or a good match for a particular search criterion – are possible, perhaps even necessary, to properly express the interpretive emphasis that individual scholars might bring to the table. What we are leveraging is the core computational affordance and transformative capacity that digital texts lend themselves so well to in order to activate not just search as the recovery of specific information but search as modulation of different models of scholarly attention.

## *Case Study: Mapping Materiality*

"Search," therefore, covers a broad set of technologies of information retrieval that model critical and interpretive perspectives. Once it ceases to be a technological black box spewing out opaque results, we can start to think about how more complex, more nuanced research questions can be articulated through such computational transformations. Algorithms, in other words, are arguments. Every time we engage with computational tools as mere tools, as some opaque process we can trust for "simple" information retrieval, not only do we attribute a dangerous neutrality to technology, we miss an opportunity to harness the power of algorithmic logic to articulate arguments of our own. In this section, I want to outline a set of attempts at modeling the changes and gradual standardization of early English orthographic practices in print. It is a phenomenon that is rather difficult, if not impossible, to observe accurately, no matter how carefully and attentively we read – in fact, one might argue that it is a problem that only properly comes into view at scale.[95]

---

[95] I will focus here mostly on the computational and scalable aspects of the problem. For a detailed discussion of the wider cultural and critical contexts, see Anupam Basu, "'Ill Shapen Sounds, and False Orthography': A Computational Approach to Early English Orthographic Variation," in *New Technologies in*

Scholars have long had opinions about the processes and forces that caused orthographic change in English that eventually lead to standardization. These theories, I shall argue, reveal certain humanistic biases about the kinds of causality and agency that drive cultural – and textual – change. By attempting to model, first by simple querying – search as information recovery – and then by building models of increasing technical sophistication and abstraction, I shall try to articulate an alternative and deeply materialistic history of the evolution of early modern printed English. There are several dimensions to the problem of tracking and pinpointing the reasons for orthographic change. Early modern orthoepists – rhetoricians, grammarians, and educators such as Sir Thomas Smith, John Hart, Richard Mulcaster, William Bullokar, Alexander Gil, and Sir John Cheke – were invested in spelling as part of a broad set of debates about national identity, the nature of cultural change, normativity, the relationship between vernacular traditions and foreign influence. Termed the "inkhorn" controversy, this debate persisted from the mid-sixteenth to the mid-seventeenth century and resulted in several published works, some of which put forward extensive guidelines for the development and standardization of English orthographic practice.[96]

Modern scholars – mostly linguists and, to a lesser extent, historians of print culture and the book – have been interested in processes of linguistic change that lead to the emergence of standardized English spelling and have speculated on the cultural and material currents that have driven this change.

*Medieval and Renaissance Studies*, ed. Laura Estill, Michael Ullyot, and Diane Jakacki (Tempe: Arizona Center for Medieval and Renaissance Studies, 2016), 167–200. For an example of leveraging computational observations about orthographic standardization to study poetic style, see Anupam Basu and Joseph Loewenstein, "Spenser's Spell: Archaism and Historical Stylometrics," *Spenser Studies* 33 (2019): 63–102.

[96] See, for example, John Hart, *An Orthographie Conteyning the Due Order and Reason, Howe to Write or Paint Thimage of Mannes Voice, Most like to the Life or Nature* (London: William Seres, 1569); William Bullokar, *Bullokars Booke at Large, for the Amendment of Orthographie for English Speech* (London: Henrie Denham, 1580); Charles Butler, *An English Grammar* (Oxford: William Turner, 1633).

But both their methodologies and their conclusions reveal more about dominant scholarly frameworks than about the ability of these methods to explain the phenomenon of orthographic change and standardization. First, in the absence of large-scale datasets, most traditional scholarship on this topic has been conducted in the form of comparative longitudinal studies of small samples from texts that were printed in multiple editions. For instance, N. F. Blake's seminal study, held to be authoritative for a long time, compared passages from five editions of *Reynard the Fox* printed between 1481 and 1550. Apart from, and perhaps due to, such a narrow historical scope for comparison, the general scholarly consensus has been that English spelling is generally nonstandardized until the decades of the Civil War and, after that, rapidly evolves to reach a more regular state that largely overlaps modern spelling. Secondly, scholarly attempts to explain how and why orthographic variation happens in early modern print reveal something about our ingrained perspectives and biases. Having claimed that spelling evolves from chaos to order around the mid-seventeenth century, most scholars seek to explain such change in one of two ways: overwhelmingly, they associate such change with the influence of the orthoepists and the inkhorn debates; and they suggest a secondary set of influences may have been the role of major widely available texts – *The Book of Common Prayer*, *The King James Bible*, and the Shakespeare *First Folio* are all mentioned as possible influences.[97] This is a deeply humanistic notion of cultural agency – that authority lies in authors, texts, and institutions. It is a model that is historicist but perhaps suffers from the same propensity of selective, anecdotal evidence that is often levied as a charge against the New Historicism. It attends to materiality but tacitly assumes that materiality comes into our view in ways that are necessarily causally traceable and mediated by conscious human agency and influence. The accepted account of the evolution of orthography echoes preconceptions about culture as an ultimately organized, directed system progressing from chaos to order in traceable ways.

---

[97] For the most comprehensive survey of this scholarship, see Vivian Salmon, "Orthography and Punctuation," in *The Cambridge History of the English Language, 1476–1776*, ed. Roger Lass (Cambridge: Cambridge University Press, 2000), 13–55.

These observations and the resulting explanations are flawed in several ways. Let us look at the data. Figure 16 shows time-series plots of orthographic variations involving the graphemes "u"/"v" – "loue"/"love" and "haue"/"have." Strangely, unlike the narrative that claims that English spelling was unstructured in the sixteenth century and any spelling form was acceptable until it was finally standardized, this graph shows surprising evidence of structure. Of course, variant spellings exist in early modern texts, at times even within the scope of the same text or page. However, it cannot be claimed that, before standardization, spelling was solely a matter of whimsy. There are strong conventional pressures here – evidence for the overwhelming preference for "u" forms before a sudden shift and ultimate complete cross-over between the 1620s and 1640s. While the time of change might not look that far off from the general scholarly consensus, the plot in Figure 17 might give us pause. The change of "y" to "i" happens in a similar structured manner, but at a completely different time – in the 1560s. A few more queries confirm that, like the "u"/"v" change, the vast majority of words that undergo this grapheme transformation follow this same pattern and time period. Figures 18 and 19 gather similar evidence for other graphemes. Perhaps especially surprising is the pattern seen for the trailing "e" in Figure 19. Many experienced readers of early modern texts would identify the trailing "e" as a characteristic of sixteenth-century spelling. However, it turns out that the pattern was not at all prevalent before the 1550s. It enters print practice in a structured manner and dies out in an equally distinctive pattern about a century later. Human readers, even highly trained and attentive ones, are not often equipped to pay attention to such subtle patterns that emerge over time dispersed through a large textual field. But once we have the scale of EEBO-TCP, these relatively simple queries for a handful of sample words make it abundantly clear that the received wisdom about several aspects of orthographic evolution in English print has been wrong. First, and most importantly, there is no general movement from simple, unregulated chaos to order. Spelling evolves in phases and at the level of graphemes. Moreover, these changes have little correlation to the debates on orthography as part of the inkhorn controversy – they begin well before the first texts that propose

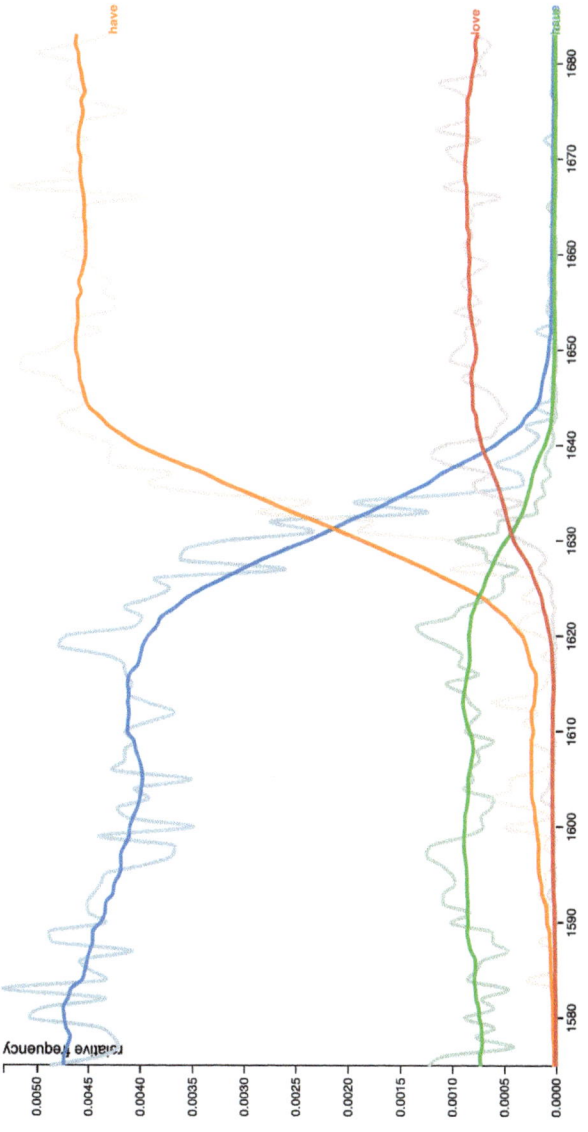

Figure 17 The change from "u" to "v." The x axis denotes year and the y axis denotes the relative frequency (i.e. the proportion of a word among the total number of words).

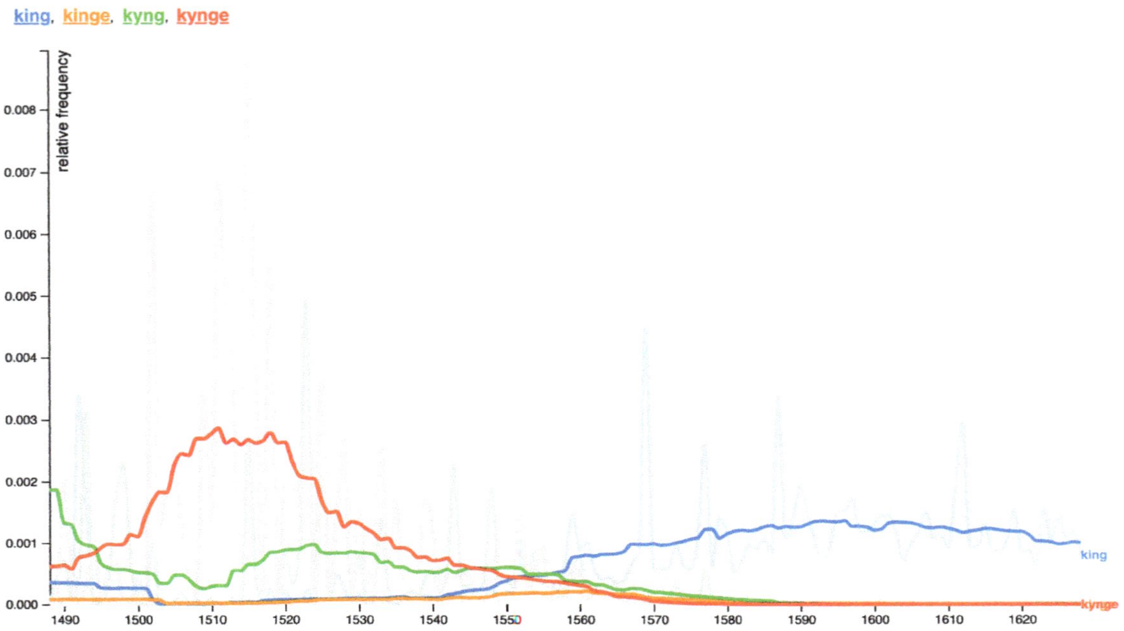

**king**, **kinge**, **kyng**, **kynge**

Figure 18 The change from "y" to "i."

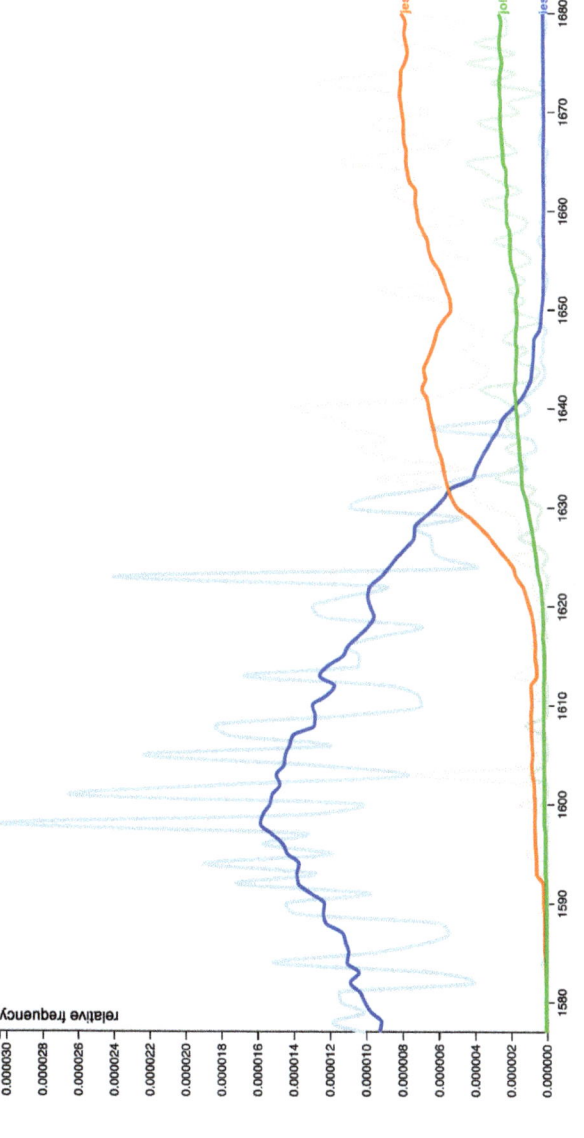

Figure 19 The change from "i" to "j".

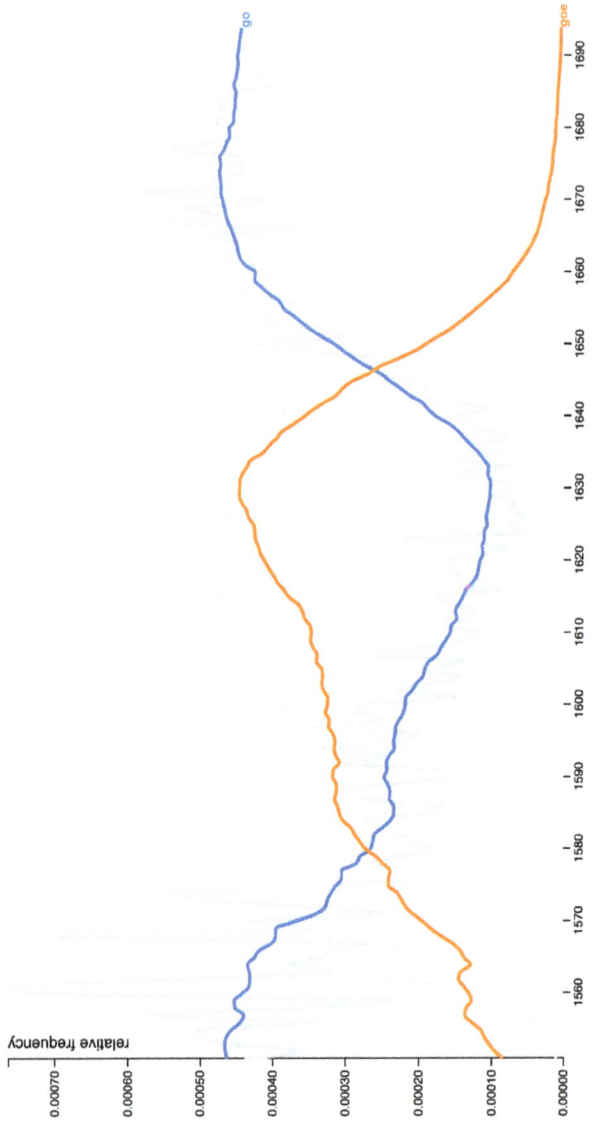

Figure 20 The emergence and eventual disappearance of the trailing "e."

orthographic protocols and have little or no correspondence to the actual changes recommended by these authors.

Thus far, we have used the scale of data only for search – as simple, unambiguous information retrieval – to verify certain claims. Even that proves to be quite powerful: it gives us a map of how orthographic change happens, albeit one that is still restricted to the evidence of several dozen words we might be able to think of as we test this hunch. A structured view of the entire field of change, however, would require some computational modeling of the problem. If the change cannot be attributed to the recommendations of the orthoepists, or the influence of a few "major" texts, why does such change happen? T. H. Howard-Hill put forward a radically original hypothesis: what we are seeing, he says, has little or nothing to do with prescriptive recommendations and is mostly a function of repetition and muscle memory![98] He argues that, unlike in France and elsewhere, there are no organized efforts at orthographic standardizations in the form of spelling manuals, dictionaries, and related reference works in England. Typesetters mostly stick to their own habits and preferences and are more interested in efficiency – and thus speed in churning out higher volumes of texts – than some ideal of standardization which might need methodical attentiveness. This charge is not surprising when one remembers that grumpy authors complaining about lax printers making mistakes is almost a minor subgenre of early modern prefatory materials.[99] But there are other material pressures at play in the print shop. Typesetting is a highly structured and repetitive process. It involved the setting of pages and, after they had served their purpose and been printed, the redistribution of type back into cases. This second task was more likely to be performed by apprentices, while typesetters were usually more experienced workers and journeymen. Over the course of thousands of pages of type set, printed, and redistributed, certain standardizations emerged. Redistribution would have become

---

[98] T. H. Howard-Hill, "Early Modern Printers and the Standardization of English Spelling," *The Modern Language Review* 101, no. 1 (2006): 16–29.

[99] For a discussion of the material processes of book production, see Adam Smyth, *Material Texts in Early Modern England* (Cambridge: Cambridge University Press, 2018).

a channel for the passing of "information" or "knowledge" from typesetters to distributors, thus establishing certain preferences and, eventually, the emergence of house styles. There would have been, moreover, an incentive for reducing wild spelling variation because not having to look at each letter while redistributing leads to a much more efficient process. Scholars including Hoard-Hill have speculated that this might explain to a large extent why variation in spelling is not as wide in the sixteenth century as scholars had previously suspected. Finally, we might enter the slightly more familiar mode of book history by considering the institutional and infrastructural pressures and incentives that might have contributed to standardization and efficiency, including periods when new type was introduced, the Stationers' Company receiving charter in 1557 and the resulting formal organization of the print trade, and the increasing volumes of print approaching the civil-war period putting greater pressure on print-shop personnel to complete their projects with efficiency.[100] What emerges from this wide-ranging (though admittedly speculative) account of orthographic standardization is a vision that is deeply attentive to the materialities and processes of print as a practice. It emphasizes internal pressures and efficiency over a dogmatic adherence to the primacy of prescriptive processes. A conception of culture, in other words, that emphasizes process over individuals, structure over intentional agency. From Althusser's structural causality to Bourdieu's field, this mode of thinking is not unfamiliar to us after a century and a half of Marxist and materialist theory, but it is definitely something that challenges our almost instinctive gravitation to actors, agents, and clearly articulated causal relations in our accounts of textual change and transmission.

How can computation help us engage with this immensely complex account of orthographic evolution? Essentially, what such an account of cultural change requires us to do is to map habits that we have little

---

[100] One instance where there is relatively clear evidence of institutional changes affecting orthographic practice in England is the improvement of standardization that results from the imposition of restrictions on hiring foreign journeymen in the early sixteenth century. See Basu, "'Ill Shapen Sounds, and False Orthography'," 177.

documentation for, the effects of repetition and muscle memory in actions that are substantially irrecoverable to us. All we have are the aggregative, accumulated effects of those actions: 65,000 texts and 1.7 billion words of "evidence." But before we model these texts, we might ask if modern statistical and computational theory gives us possible ways to understand the kind of phenomena we are likely observing here – large-scale, autonomous, and structured emergence developing out of the accumulated reiterations of millions of individual actions, each by itself unrestricted and independent, but adding up to distinctive overall patterns.[101] Much recent work in statistical theory, as well as, increasingly, in the philosophy of computation, has paid attention to such formation of structure out of individual action without central organization.[102] Described variously as emergence, collective intelligence, or swarm theory, such models try to describe highly structured but essentially stochastic, unpredictable phenomena in terms of the patterns and transitions they produce. The most accessible example of such phenomena are swarms of living creatures such as fish or birds, but emergence as a model of causation and change is increasingly being applied to a variety of complex phenomena from the development of crystals to the organization of neural pathways. There is no

---

[101] Emergence, broadly understood as the formation of autonomous, large-scale structure as the aggregated result of microscale individual actions, has drawn considerable attention in recent years. For discussions of it at the intersections of philosophy, computer science, and cultural studies, see Mark A. Bedau and Paul Humphreys, eds., *Emergence: Contemporary Readings in Philosophy and Science* 1st ed. (Cambridge, MA: MIT Press, 2008); Manuel (London)

[102] For statistical discussions of collective intelligence, see Thomas W. Malone and Michael S. Bernstein, eds., *Handbook of Collective Intelligence* (Cambridge MA: MIT Press, 2015); and Mohd Nadhir Ab Wahab, Samia Nefti-Meziani, and Adham Atyabi, "A Comprehensive Review of Swarm Optimization Algorithms," ed. Catalin Buiu, *PLOS ONE* 10, no. 5 (2015), https://doi.org/10.1371/journal.pone.0122827. More philosophical and cultural dimensions are covered in N. Katherine Hayles, "Chaos and Poststructuralism," in *Chaos Bound: Orderly Disorder in Contemporary Literature and Science* (Cornell, NY: Cornell University Press, 1990), 175–208, www.jstor.org/stable/10.7591/j.ctt207g6w4.10; and DeLanda, *Philosophy and Simulation*.

premeditated plan in such swarms, nor any central organization by a leader who makes prescriptions or sets the agenda. Instead, each individual member of the immense collective takes relatively simple actions dictated by individual preferences and the interests of local efficiency – trying to get into the middle of a group of one's neighbors to be safe, for example. And, out of the aggregated repetition of innumerable such individual actions that each articulate both a degree of randomness and certain patterned constraints, emerge the massive and highly intricate structures we see.

But does this lesson from nature translate to culture?[103] To ask this question, we must first be able to represent quantitatively the "habits" of spelling represented in a given chunk of text. I approached this by drawing 100,000 random samples of 5,000-word chunks from the corpus. Each chunk is then broken down into a series of letter n-grams.[104] N-grams are usually sequences of words of length "n" that are used widely in natural language-processing algorithms. However, since spelling change happens, as we have seen, mostly at the level of graphemes, we use letter- instead of word-level n-grams and dissect words into 1-, 2-, and 3-letter sequences, keeping track, as well, of the beginnings and ends of words. This yields a massive table of 100,000 rows and approximately 30,000 columns – each row being a vector representing the orthographic habits that characterize a particular sample of text over a feature space of 30,000 letter n-grams from which we can select the 200 most salient features or graphemes that encapsulate the most distinctive patterns of change over the first two centuries of English print. Once this somewhat involved set of operations is done, we can then generate a visual projection of orthographic habits. Generated using a technique called principal component analysis (PCA), what this field represents, in essence, are different locations where different orthographic

---

[103] It is well beyond the scope of this discussion, but the depiction of the terror of swarms in science fiction gives us a glimpse of the fundamentally unsettling and uncanny ways in which such models invite us to think about structure and "intelligence" while letting go of our preconceptions about agency: Robin R. Murphy, "Swarm Robots in Science Fiction," *Science Robotics* 6, no. 56 (July 28, 2021).

[104] For details of this process, see Basu and Loewenstein, "Spenser's Spell," 81.

tendencies gather. Figure 21 shows this space inhabited by the 200 most salient graphemes. The graph plots scores for principal components 1 and 2 on the x and y axes, but what we must attend to more closely are the locations of individual graphemes. For a sample of text, each grapheme may be thought of as exerting a gravitational pull on the sample toward its position in the field. The strength of this gravitation is proportional to the preponderance of that grapheme in the text. In other words, a text that largely prefers "i" graphemes over "y" graphemes will tend to be pulled to the third quadrant in the top left corner and so forth. Each text will be situated somewhere in this two-dimensional field as a result of how these 200 orthographic features are distributed within it.

With this basic technical infrastructure in place, we are finally ready to explore the evolution of orthographic habits over time. There are several ways to use this data to demonstrate what we had suspected from the somewhat arbitrary samples of individual words – that words sharing similar graphemic patterns change together.[105] However, at present, our focus is not on the fact that early orthography is more structured than generally thought, but on the question of whether such change could emerge over time as the result of habits formed during the repetitive processes of the printing press. In order to plot this orthographic landscape at a given moment in time, we take the PCA space generated in Figure 21 and lay it down as a flat surface. This horizontal plane represents schematically what we might think of as the field of orthographic habits and biases – the metaphor of "field" for thinking about the organization of cultural habits aligns well with this representation of different regimens of orthography as different locations on a plane. For each year, we gather text samples, analyze their orthographic profiles, and then situate each text in some position on this horizontal plane that represents principal components 1 and 2 from Figure 21. This adds a third dimension: a z-axis, or what we might think of as the contour of this landscape. Locations on the field representing habits that are dominant at a particular time gain elevation and turn into hills, and habits that fall out of favor are represented by troughs or

---

[105] For a detailed visualization and explanation of this phenomenon, see Basu and Loewenstein, "Spenser's Spell," 86.

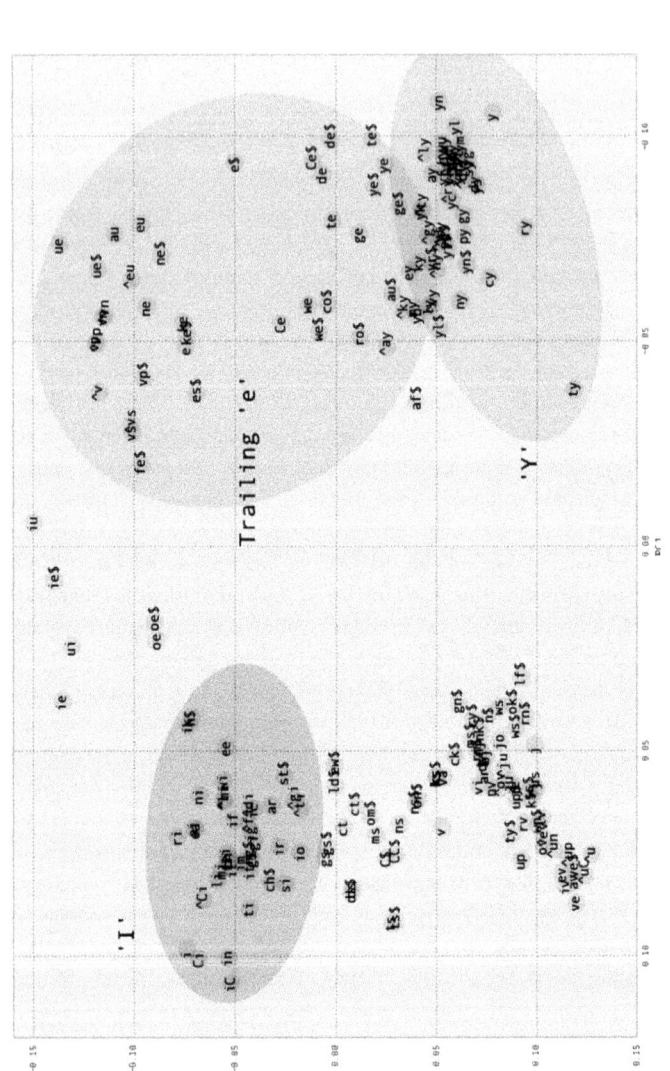

Figure 21 The 200 most salient orthographic features mapped in PCA space.

valleys. Because almost all texts in the corpus are dateable to a very short year range, we can create such contoured landscape profiles for each year. Now, if the distribution of habits over time were to evolve relatively unevenly – that is, if changes from year to year were to show significantly divergent profiles – we would have little justification to claim that we are witnessing emergent behavior. But if, on the other hand, variations from year to year produce smooth and gradual changes that, in aggregate, reveal the emergence and evolution of highly structured overall patterns, it would indicate that orthographic habits are quite likely to be the result of such accumulative behavior.

Since we are interested in changes from year to year, this series of visualizations is ideally viewed as an animation or interactive video. Figures 22–28 show plots for 1500, 1550, 1575, 1600, 1625, 1650, and 1675 to give a general sense of the gradual but ultimately highly structured and distinctive development of patterns. We should remember that the number of texts per year in the first half of the sixteenth century is relatively small, and this, combined with quite a high degree of orthographic variation, makes the field very rough and uneven. There's no clear distinctive shape to the landscape, and lots of small hills and valleys exist in close proximity. In other words, what we are seeing are several competing and contradictory conventions struggling for hegemony. Over time, however, much more distinctive patterns emerge, and by 1575 it is clear that a major shift in orthographic paradigms has been underway for a while, patterns that are consolidated by the early seventeenth century. It is possible to look more closely into exactly what norms drive these patterns by looking at the matrix of features for each year or mapping this pattern as a heatmap on the two-dimensional plot of Figure 20, but plotting this as a contour map allows us to focus on the process of transition better. We can still tell broad patterns and anomalies quite clearly, however. For example, the graph for 1625 marks the second great period of upheaval in spelling after the 1560s. However, as many spellings are in flux and beginning to switch over to more modern forms, the solitary spike between the first and fourth quadrants represents the perhaps somewhat unexpected insistence on using the trailing "e," a fashion that soon enters precipitous decline, as the complete demolition of that hill by 1650 attests. By 1675, the great paradigm shift away from sixteenth-century spelling convention is complete,

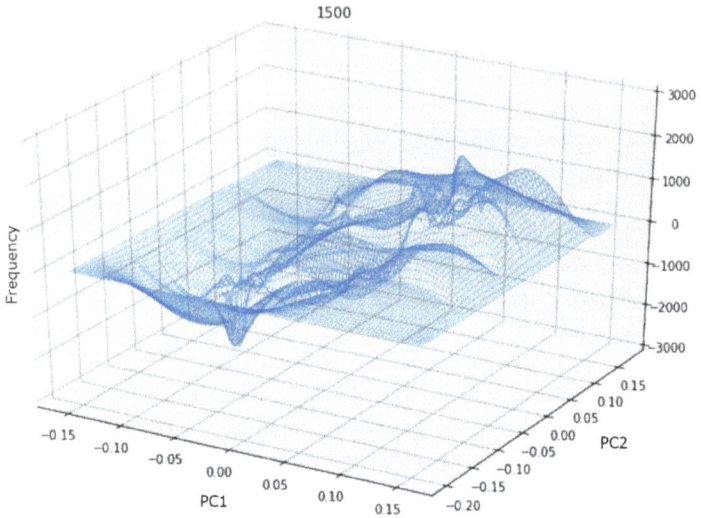

Figures 22–28 The horizontal plane on these visualizations represents the principal components from Figure 20 laid flat, as it were. The x axis represents PC1, the y axis PC2. As in Figure 20, each area of this xy plane represents a particular spelling habit. For example, the lower right quadrant gathers examples of "y" while "i" tends to gather in the upper left. The vertical, or z-axis, represents the frequencies of such graphemes for a given year. If a spelling habit is quite frequent, we get a hill – if it becomes very rare, we get a valley. So it is to be expected that when, by 1675, the spelling of words such as "kyng" have evolved to "king," etcetera, the upper left will have a hill while the lower right will turn into a valley. The entirety of the landscape together represents multiple facets of orthographic habit and the degree to which they become stable over time.

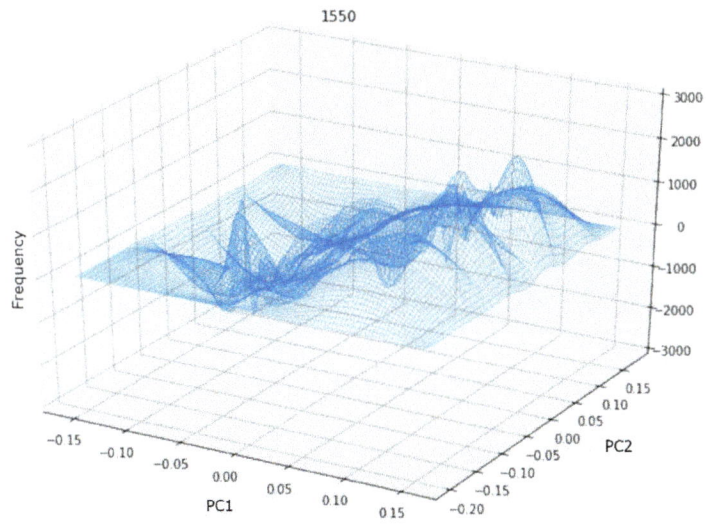
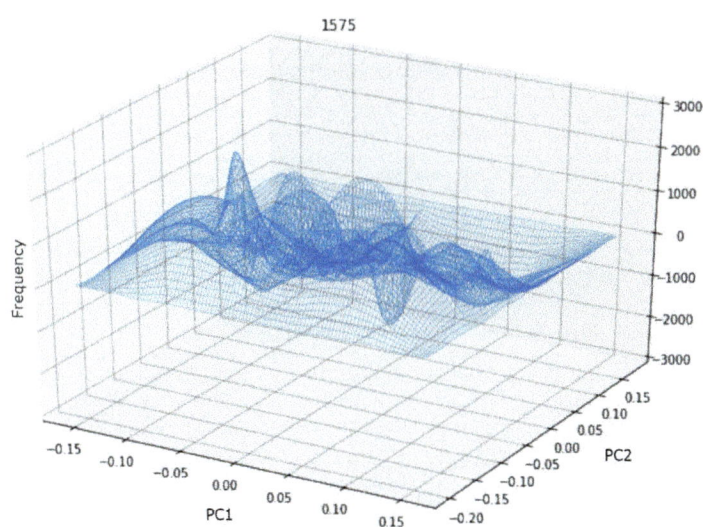

Figures 22–28 (Cont.)

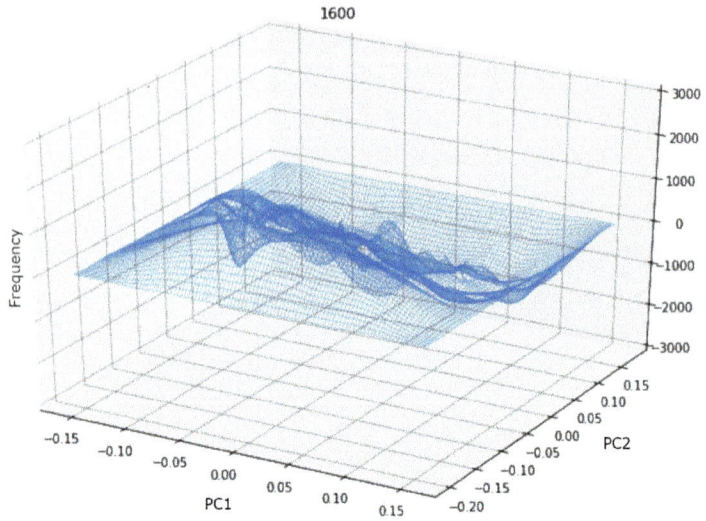

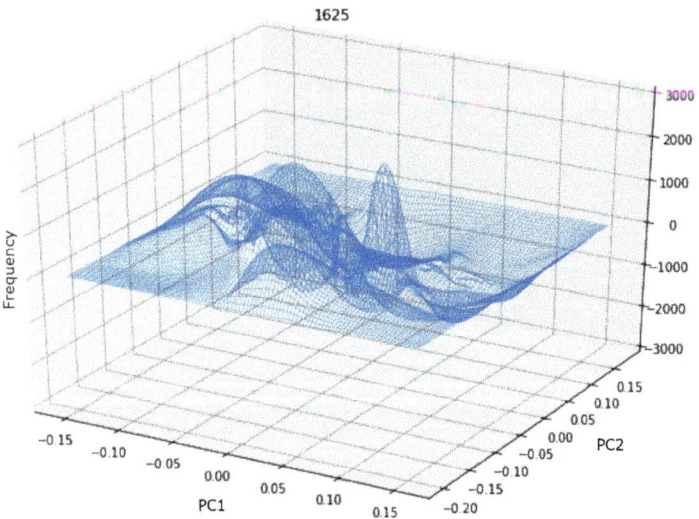

Figures 22–28 (Cont.)

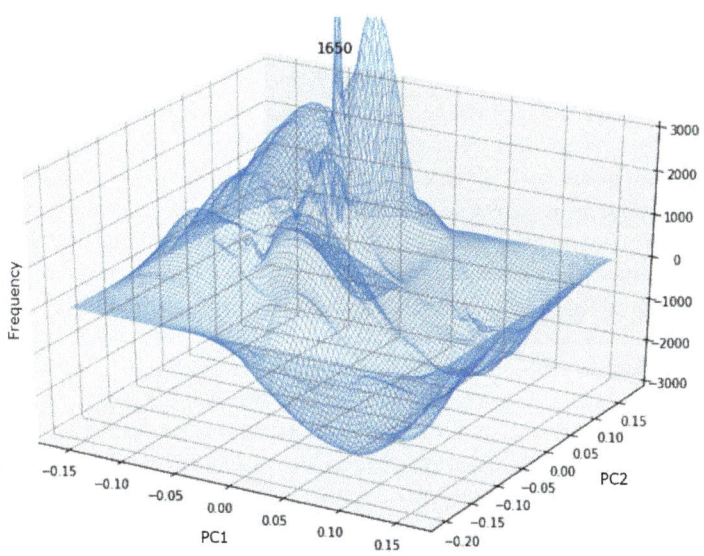

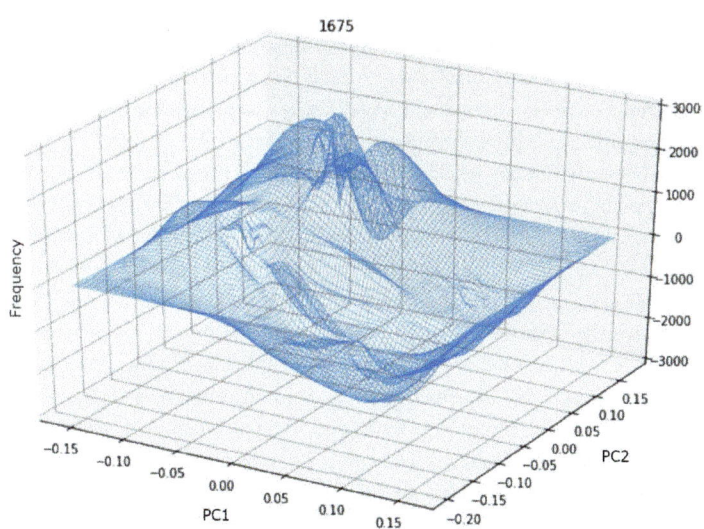

Figures 22–28 (Cont.)

and the landscape settles into a relatively calm set of undulations with well-established habits or hills, and equally well-defined valleys.

The techniques and visualizations in this case study will prove challenging for many humanists. I would suggest, however, that the real obstacle posed by such an approach is not technical but conceptual. It lies not so much in navigating the technological interface (substantial as it is) as in articulating a deeply humanistic problem in unfamiliar quantitative, statistical, and scalable terms. The account of orthographic change that emerges in the aforementioned experiments is a fundamentally materialist one – a model that locates cultural change as much in the mechanical processes of the printing press and the repetitive economies of habit as in institutional or individual agency. Culture, we are reminded, is visceral and embodied as much as it is intellectual. The vantage point of scale allows us to see the contours of the habituated patterns accrued over decades, over millions of repetitive actions, each insignificant and unconscious in itself, but adding up to a distinctively structured tapestry. In fact, the problem itself emerges only once we attain the vantage point of scale – when we can query time-series data spread over more than two centuries (Figures 16–19). These graphs are fairly straightforward representations of data, but they evoke a set of interesting questions that require further modeling and interpretive deformance. The first time I ran a search for the token "loue," I wasn't expecting such a distinctive shape. But the simple question it raised – "I wonder why this pattern happens" – led to a series of increasingly involved queries and, eventually, models.

Whether or not our scholarship is particularly invested in the evolution of orthography, I hope this set of experiments invites us to rethink conceptual and categorical boundaries: between the micromechanics of encultured and embodied habit and the accumulated emergence of cultural patterns; between the tractable surfaces of individual texts we navigate so easily and the vast sea of interconnected textual tapestry that forms the cultural record. We often get so caught up with computation as a series of technical tools to master that the immense possibilities of computation as mode of thought and of scale as perspective remain beyond our framework. Digital work, it is important to remember, is fundamentally collaborative. From curators to technical support staff assisting projects – there are many ways to negotiate the technological challenges. But thinking about culture in scalable computational terms requires us, in turn, to think about computation as something that can move beyond rigid empiricism and accommodate open-ended play and generative speculation – something that can not only lend itself to humanistic modes of thinking but enhance them. I have argued that the task of the curator is not only to make texts accessible but to invite us, to teach us, to think about scale – to think of the corpus not only as a collection of individual texts that are not only accessible through familiar modes of critical attention, but from a fundamentally scalable perspective as well.

\*

These case studies, I hope, hold up certain concrete possibilities for research and pedagogy for Shakespearean scholars – ways in which both speculative search and large-scale stylometric analysis may be integrated into our work. Computational thinking is fundamentally intertextual. We should ask ourselves how it might help us move from the granularity of close reading to the wider horizons of style, genre, oeuvre, and canon. Search – not merely as an out-of-the-box tool, but as a mode of open-ended exploration – should be as much a part of our classrooms and research workflows as a dictionary or a thesaurus. Imagine the difference between looking up an unfamiliar early modern usage such as "marry!" in a dictionary or an editorial footnote and being able to use even a simple search tool like collocation to see it in context used in dozens of comedies in particular social registers. What would it be like to think about genre from the very outset as a collective, intertextual, fluid, and evolving phenomenon – more interesting in its interstices and exceptions than in its staid canonical exemplars?[106] The comparative and intertextual perspective that allows us to build orthographic and stylistic profiles might be leveraged to analyze compositorial hands or authorial influence. Compositorial analysis has been crucial to scholars of Shakespeare's early

---

[106] See, for example, the computational exploration of *Othello* as a play whose rhetorical patterns seem distinctive from the other great Shakespearean tragedies and show affinities to the language of comedy, in Jonathan Hope and Michael Witmore, "The Hundredth Psalm to the Tune of 'Green Sleeves': Digital Approaches to Shakespeare's Language of Genre," *Shakespeare Quarterly* 61, no. 3 (2010): 357–90.

editions but has rarely been applied in such detail to other authors. Spenser's texts, for instance, have been shown to have distinctive orthographic profiles – for example, in the commentary in the *Shepheardes Calendar* or the two editions of the *Faerie Queene*.[107] To model such questions, we need to move beyond the notion of computation as mere techne and embrace it as a means of persuasion capable of accommodating humanistic conceptions of cultural change.

If there is to be a "computational turn" in the humanities, it cannot function based on a split between dry technical virtuosity and qualitative nuance. Neither should technology be relegated to the role of answering questions or confirming hunches that are raised through qualitative methods. Only when we can *think* with and through technology – when we can accommodate stochastic play as easily as we accommodate hermeneutic ambiguity – will technology and scale become first-order participants in humanistic inquiry.

---

[107] See Basu and Loewenstein, "Spenser's Spell."

# Cambridge Elements⹅

## Shakespeare and Text

### Claire M. L. Bourne
*The Pennsylvania State University*

Claire M. L. Bourne is Associate Professor of English at The Pennsylvania State University. She is author of *Typographies of Performance in Early Modern England* (Oxford University Press 2020) and editor of the collection *Shakespeare / Text* (Bloomsbury 2021). She has published extensively on early modern book design and reading practices in venues such as *PBSA*, *ELR*, *Shakespeare*, and numerous edited collections. She is also co-author (with Jason Scott-Warren) of an article attributing the annotations in the Free Library of Philadelphia's copy of the Shakespeare First Folio to John Milton. She has edited Fletcher and Massinger's *The Sea Voyage* for the *Routledge Anthology of Early Modern Drama* (2020) and is working on an edition of *Henry the Sixth, Part 1* for the Arden Shakespeare, Fourth Series.

### Rory Loughnane
*University of Kent*

Rory Loughnane is Reader in Early Modern Studies and Co-director of the Centre for Medieval and Early Modern Studies at the University of Kent. He is the author or editor of nine books and has published widely on Shakespeare and textual studies. In his role as Associate Editor of the New Oxford Shakespeare, he has edited more than ten of Shakespeare's plays, and co-authored with Gary Taylor a book-length study about the 'Canon and Chronology' of Shakespeare's works. He is a General Editor of the forthcoming

Oxford Marlowe edition, a Series Editor of Studies in Early
Modern Authorship (Routledge), a General Editor of the
*CADRE* database (cadredb.net), and a General Editor of The
Revels Plays series (Manchester University Press).

ADVISORY BOARD

Patricia Akhimie
*The Folger Institute*
Terri Bourus
*Florida State University*
Dennis Britton
*University of British
   Columbia*
Miles P. Grier
*Queen's College,
   City University
   of New York*
Chiaki Hanabusa
*Keio University*
Sujata Iyengar
*University of Georgia*
Jason Scott-Warren
*University of Cambridge*

M. J. Kidnie
*University of Western Ontario*
Zachary Lesser
*University of Pennsylvania*
Tara L. Lyons
*Illinois State University*
Joyce MacDonald
*University of Kentucky*
Laurie Maguire
*Magdalen College, University
   of Oxford*
David McInnis
*University of Melbourne*
Iolanda Plescia
*Sapienza – University of Rome*
Alan Stewart
*Columbia University*

## About the Series

Cambridge Elements in Shakespeare and Text offers a platform for
original scholarship about the creation, circulation, reception,
remaking, use, performance, teaching, and translation of the
Shakespearean text across time and place. The series seeks to publish
research that challenges–and pushes beyond–the conventional
parameters of Shakespeare and textual studies.

# Cambridge Elements ≡

## Shakespeare and Text

ELEMENTS IN THE SERIES

*Shakespeare, Malone and the Problems of Chronology*
Tiffany Stern

*Theatre History, Attribution Studies, and the Question of Evidence*
Holger Schott Syme

*Facsimiles and the History of Shakespeare Editing*
Paul Salzman

*Editing Archipelagic Shakespeare*
Rory Loughnane and Willy Maley

*Shakespeare Broadcasts and the Question of Value*
Beth Sharrock

*Shakespeare and Scale: The Archive of Early Printed English*
Anupam Basu

A full series listing is available at: www.cambridge.org/ESTX

For EU product safety concerns, contact us at Calle de José Abascal, 56–1°, 28003 Madrid, Spain or eugpsr@cambridge.org.

www.ingramcontent.com/pod-product-compliance
Ingram Content Group UK Ltd.
Pitfield, Milton Keynes, MK11 3LW, UK
UKHW021825180425
457535UK00012B/105